LIFE
CHALLENGE
ASTROLOGY
karmic indicators in the birthchart

LIFE
CHALLENGE
ASTROLOGY
karmic indicators in the birthchart

RICHARD
STRAUSS

SAMUEL WEISER, INC.
York Beach, Maine

First published in 1989 by
Samuel Weiser, Inc.
Box 612
York Beach, Maine 03910

Library of Congress Cataloging in Publication Data

Strauss, Richard.
    Life-challenge astrology.

    1. Astrology.   2. Horoscopes.   I. Title.
BF1708.1.S83   1989   133.5   88–33874
ISBN 0–87728–668–X

Cover illustration by Michael Martin after a design by Jennifer Jones.
Typeset in 12 point Bembo
Printed in the United States of America

Contents

Acknowledgments

I would like to thank Jeanne Corner, who gave me the encouragement and support that sustained my early interest in astrology, and who intuitively foresaw the manifestation of this book.

Thanks also go to Elizabeth Holmes, whose confidence in my astrological judgment provided me with clients who were uniquely open to, and validating of, the early explorations into this approach.

Introduction

When I was a beginning student of astrology, my time and energy were devoted to understanding the individual factors that make up a horoscope. I eagerly devoured scores of books that described the signs, planets, houses, angles, aspects, configurations, etc. Doing my own chart, and those of my friends, eventually led me to see astrology as a valid language for human behavior and character, and because of my background as a clinical psychologist, I was enthusiastic about using this tool to help people.

While I dabbled in the use of the birthchart to predict wealth, relationships, children, career, etc., and used transits and progressions to pinpoint current cycles, I longed to find a way to assist others at a deeper level. I began to realize that there is little agreement among writers as to the true purpose of the horoscope. Is it merely a descriptive tool? Does it tell us specifically what to do? Does it simply inform us of what we were? Can it tell us what we should become? Does it contain the solutions to the problems it outlines? Is there a way to view it in its entirety, or is it a conglomeration of disparate parts?

I eventually became frustrated by the fact that I could only see a horoscope in pieces. There seemed to be separate "clumps" of significance which, while devastatingly accurate as symbols describing personality, did not relate to each other clearly. Intuition told me that there must be an overall cohesiveness in a chart, a "story" that would give perspective to an individual's life. In addition, I believed that such a concept might clarify the horoscope's role as a statement of past, present, and future, and provide a developmental perspective. For a long time I struggled to find a concept which would reveal such a story.

The purpose of this book is to explain a concept which I feel satisfies this search, to describe the part each astrological factor plays in the story, and to outline a technique of synthesis by which the nature of this story may be discovered.

1

The Life-Challenge Concept

One afternoon I was studying my birthchart as I had done many times before, straining to pull all the pieces together by darting my attention from one section, or group of planets, to another. At the same time, I kept in mind the qualities of my character and the way my life had developed to that point. I tried to remain open to a new synthesis, to avoid a partial interpretation of the chart. Although I sometimes gained new information about myself during these sessions, I invariably felt frustrated that I could not perceive some overall theme.

Suddenly I saw the factors of my chart organized along a polar axis in a pattern that described a developmental direction in my life. Looking at the factors in the chart in this way, I could see why I had been a certain type of person in my early life, and what qualities I was developing as I grew older and became a fuller, more rounded person. I realized in an instant why life had presented me with certain relationships and experiences as challenges to grow in certain ways. I felt clarified, disconcerted (by the challenge being revealed to me), and excited (at the possibilities for understanding), all at the same time.

As I continued studying my chart I realized that this central concept was reinforced by every sign placement, house placement, and planetary aspect. While my ideas about my chart have changed over the years, due to refinements in my approach, my basic perspective on all birth charts was born in that instant.

I eagerly approached the charts of everyone I knew and in each case I found a perspective that had similar implications to my own. The charts confirmed that the developmental directions I described accounted for the growth that had occurred in these individuals' lives. My friends and clients could not deny the validity of the characterization. My search for a synthesizing concept was ended.

I think what impressed me most about this experience was seeing that there is a Higher Intelligence in our lives, one which gracefully leads us (in cooperation with our various independent choices) toward expansion and growth. The relative comfort or discomfort of this process depends on whether the lower self embraces or resists these choices. Hopefully, using the approach I am about to outline, which I call Life-Challenge astrology, will enable us to integrate the inevitable changes in our lives consciously.

Before getting into the specific astrological factors themselves, I would like to discuss some of the broader implications of my approach. I have concluded that each of us is born with a core of character traits and tendencies which I call a Karmic Inheritance. Most of us have noticed individual differences in children right from birth. Intuitively, we know they cannot be accounted for by environmental factors. As a parent, I have frequently noted that my personality was being impacted (in terms of change) more by my daughter than hers was by me! There is strength and consistency in this inherited character, which implies to me that a long development has gone into its formation.

It appears to me that this core of qualities can be characterized by a certain theme or style, as is done in various typological systems. One person can be called an extrovert; another an introvert. We can be considered primarily mental, emotional, or physical. We all resort to these categories to "sum up" other individuals.

The fact that we can nearly always do this suggests something important to me: we are typically imbalanced in our approach to life. Especially in the first half of our lives, we tend to animate certain tendencies and characteristics that get "dealt with" by life. This Karmic Inheritance (the word "karma" is used deliberately to reveal the problematic nature of these tendencies) is seen to be a limited package of behaviors with which to meet life's challenges. Most of us can see as we get older that we have developed fuller responses to life, a wider range of qualities which enable us to be appropriate in many different situations whereas, in our youth, we would have called up a more limited, familiar, habitual behavior pattern.

It should be noted that the Inheritance provides us with our best qualities as well, since we have developed them into a permanent personality style. We "specialize" in them, and "rely" on them in presenting ourselves favorably. The problem here is that we come to depend on a limited behavioral repertoire.

This is where the Life-Challenge comes in. Whether we like it or not, life inevitably seems to create circumstances that require new responses. Most people can think of situations and relationships that were reluctantly suffered, yet later proved to be profoundly valuable as opportunities for growth. I believe these lessons are not accidents but rather can be seen as examples of the Life-Challenge. In my experience, the Karmic Inheritance and Life-Challenge have an oppositional relationship to each other.

Apparently, the former group develops in one direction, then crystallizes in its structure, requiring the power of a polar force to move us "off the dime" toward continued growth.

I have learned to see in the birthchart both the nature of the Karmic Inheritance and the appropriate qualities and experiences that will be brought to the individual as the Life-Challenge. The Inheritance group usually consists of a small number of chart factors (though each typically expresses itself in more than one way). The Challenge-group is made up of the rest, although some of these will play a more primary role than the others in bringing balance and versatility to our lives. While there are a few straightforward "rules" for identifying some factors in the Challenge-group (sign and house position of the North Node; signs on the Ascendant and Midheaven; most of the natural sign-equivalencies of planetary house placements), the remainder of the story requires a creative process of synthesis which we will attempt to explain in this text.

For example, let's say that you have an inheritance composed of the signs Cancer, Leo, and Libra. While these three display some differences in expression, we can recognize the common denominator in this group: strong social needs. The positive expression of this inheritance might be sensitivity to the social needs of others and appreciation for the role social approval plays in your life. The negative, or limiting, side of this inheritance (which would stimulate the need for a compensating life-challenge in another direction) could be excessive social dependency.

This process of abstract synthesis, whereby we look for the theme that expresses the broad commonality of the three signs that make up the karmic inheritance, is the key to my approach. Having determined that social dependency is the concept, we are likely to find signs representing independence and individuality, such as Aries and Aquarius, highlighted in your chart. And, if we are accurate in our analysis, we will find that you were more likely to accommodate others, to try to fit into the group, and to seek approval from peers when you were younger. It is likely that you did not develop fully your unique potential due to an over-sensitivity to cues from others. In later life, perhaps in response to progressions and transits involving Mars or Uranus, you may have found yourself being assertive and individualistic in a new way.

Often new behaviors elicited by the life-challenge are expressed in an extreme and clumsy way. Since they are relatively unintegrated, we seem to exaggerate them for awhile, perhaps to make sure we do not abandon the attempt and fall back into the old, familiar inheritance. For example, with your Cancer, Leo, Libra inheritance, you may compensate for your social dependency by being overly aggressive, eccentric, and rebellious for a period in your life. Your destiny would be to become comfortable enough with your life-challenge to express either end of the polarity appropriately and gracefully, depending upon the demands of the situation. Thus, in maturity, you could cooperate in a group effort, but also retain your assertiveness and individuality.

Why is the cosmos like this? Is there any familiar concept from philosophy or science that is consistent with this notion of how our lives unfold? I believe there is. The concept of homeostasis appears to be a satisfying explanation. It is most familiar to us as a biological phenomenon, by which our needs for balance are made known to us through a series of need-gestalts. When the body requires fuel for continued functioning, you become hungry. You are imbalanced in the direction of nutrient deficiency and usually experience two things. First, you feel the deficiency itself, a hunger pang or a distraction from what you are doing. Second, you have a fantasy of something to eat which will correct, or rebalance, your state.

If we can make an analogy at a much broader level, we can say that this principle operates at all levels of existence. The universe seeks balance, ultimately, although there are wild swings in between extreme polar expressions. I believe that a development of any extreme tendency automatically results in a tension which eventually calls forth a swing back in the other direction. This is familiar to us as a physical law: every action brings about an equal and opposite reaction.

Let's consider an application of this law at the level of karma and reincarnation. Perhaps the natural destiny of each "soul" is to achieve a balance that would be expressed as the ability to embrace all the signs of the zodiac and manifest them in their highest forms. Somewhere along the way to spiritual perfection, we learn to master Aries, Taurus, Gemini, etc., at their highest levels. Each lifetime is a learning experience in which we are continually developing higher forms of the various signs. It is my experience that the chart shows us which ones have reached a certain extreme (albeit typically immature) level of development (inheritance) and which ones are being called forth as a reaction in another direction (life-challenge) to compensate for this temporary imbalance. Perhaps we swing back and forth through lifetimes in this manner, developing ever higher and more balanced forms of expression of each sign. An image of this could be a spiral staircase where each step represents a progressively higher expression of each kind of astrological energy and the circular form corresponds to the kind of compensatory structure required for balance and integrity.

To complete our analogy, then, the phenomenon of hunger, as a need-gestalt, can parallel one at the level of karma. We sense an imbalance (karmic inheritance) which is somehow to be corrected by an appropriate reaction (life-challenge). The whole concept of karma, which we tend to moralize about and make into a personal God who sits taking notes, is really an intuition about this natural law of homeostasis. If we do not live in tune with this law of balance, we "pay" by the equal and opposite reaction of karmic "retribution." An extension of this idea, which has been helpful to me, is that truth is never to be found in any one direction along a polar axis, but rather is always a paradoxical combination (ultimately a transcendence) of both ends.

2

Overview of Planets, Signs and Houses

I do not think it is coincidence that the least controversy in astrology is over the zodiacal signs. We are continually discovering (and debating) the significance of new planets, asteroids, fixed stars, black holes, parts, midpoints, etc. We are at odds regarding the houses—their number, their cuspal calculation, their importance, and their meanings. We struggle with the issue of the parallel meanings versus the subtle distinctions between the planets, signs, and houses (not to mention the controversial rulerships). We are even divided over which zodiac best fits a certain time frame (I use the tropical zodiac). However, there seems to be little argument about the existence of twelve signs and the ultimate cyclical completion which they represent. I believe the significance of this is what underlies the life-challenge approach to chart interpretation. *The crucial knowledge to be gained from a horoscope is a broad karmic theme which takes into account all the astrological factors and which is expressed primarily in terms of a zodiacal imbalance and its compensatory dynamic challenge.*

While we will discriminate between planets, signs, and houses in terms of their contribution to this continuum, we need to assert here that their ultimate symbolic (i.e., zodiacal) meanings are interchangeable.[1] In other words, whereas one factor (e.g., a planet) may reflect a past inheritance and another (e.g., a house) may indicate a future challenge, the Moon is a Cancer factor, the Fourth House is a Cancer factor, and the sign, Cancer, is a Cancer factor.

The zodiacal theme, or developmental story, may be depicted linearly by a continuum, as illustrated in figure 1. The point of this figure is that all astrological factors in a birthchart — the planets, their aspects, the signs and houses in which they are placed, house cusps (particularly the angles), the Nodes, the Part of Fortune — contribute to an arrangement of the zodiacal energies along this continuum. By translating them into their zodiacal equivalencies, all factors in a chart can be "boiled down" to signs. It is the position of a sign relative to its dynamic effect on the balance (in terms of the inheritance-challenge axis) that is important to us, rather than simply a flat delineation of the sign's general characteristics or specific planetary functions. In this

Karmic Inheritance   Life-Challenge
Imbalance   Counter-balance

Figure 1. Developmental axis illustrating oppositional nature of inheritance and challenge. Life-development is seen to move from left to right.

---

[1]This point has been popularized, though within a different context, by Zipporah Dobyns in *Evolution Through the Zodiac* (Los Angeles: TIA Publications, 1972).

sense, there are many combinations of astrological factors that could contribute to a similar zodiacal placement on the continuum; these are secondary in importance. The planetary positions, aspects, and so forth are not so meaningful as the general theme: which energies are most distorted and which need to be cultivated in compensation.

There is a broad spectrum of possibilities for each sign based on the subtlety of human experience. It has been said often that saints suffer their faults far more acutely than average individuals due to the sensitivity of their awareness. Thus, they may be dealing with karma at a mental or emotional level that hardly reflects itself behaviorally! The important implication of this point becomes obvious when we begin to relate these ideas to astrological signs. There are many different levels of manifestation of each sign, for example. One person may mishandle Pisces energy overtly through alcoholism, while another does so internally by idealizing relationships and being constantly disappointed. The first person's recovery will have outward manifestations; the second's may involve a readjusted outlook that simply makes him or her feel better. (The way to narrow down the possible expressions of karma within each chart will be explored fully later.)

Perhaps a primitive illustration will be helpful here. Let us suppose your horoscope reveals an inheritance of, or past emphasis on, freedom and independence. You may have exploited your desire for self-determination at the expense of your relationships, your emotional stability, and the persistence required for lasting achievement. This conclusion could be based on any number of possibilities. The theme could be supported by afflicted planets (or Nodes) in Aries, Sagittarius, and Aquarius. It really doesn't matter which past-indicating factors are involved, which aspects between the planets are involved, or which houses are heavily occupied. I can say from experience, however, that the important signs at both ends of the continuum will be supported by multiple indications, rather than a single factor.

The situation is reflected in figure 2. The signs on the left are ones that are not being expressed with balance and thus are limiting and frustrating your growth. The signs on the right are those that need to be cultivated and represent a challenge. If you could be a little more emotionally dependent (Leo), more interested in partnership (Libra), and more emotionally focused (Scorpio), you would be compensating for the karmic imbalance which has developed. Again, this is an abstract, linear model. Its purpose is to emphasize the major role of the zodiacal signs as the final factors in your theme. The techniques of analyzing the individual factors contributing to the major theme in a horoscope can now be approached with increased perspective.

Planets represent the dynamic energy centers of our being, providing the thrust for our actions, feelings, and thoughts. The fact that we all have the same planets in our charts suggests that we are structured alike, that we share a fundamental nature. Each planet governs a specific form of energy. Their number accounts for the complexity of human nature. The variations in sign placement, house placement, and the aspectual relations between the planets reflect the individuality within this nature.

Karmic Inheritance   **Life-Challenge**

Aries, Sagittarius, Aquarius   Leo, Libra, Scorpio

Figure 2.   Example developmental axis expressing a life-challenge to develop some concern for what others think, for commitment in relationships, and intensity of purpose.

For awhile, I thought planets had tendencies to place themselves along the continuum according to their inherent natures.
Over the years, I have dropped this belief. Neither do the signs
have inherent tendencies to place themselves at one end of the
continuum. No sign is more karmically limiting than another.
None represents an energy which is easier to express than
another. All are equally demanding and capable of distortion.

I see the houses as usually challenging. I believe they are
typically "new" factors in each lifetime and, therefore, reflect the
right side of the developmental polar axis. A house most frequently requires a new adaptation from a planet, whether the
planet itself happens to be an old or new factor. Let's say, for
example, the Moon is a disposition inherited from the past. Its
placement in the Seventh House, however, indicates that the
individual needs to learn how to adapt that disposition to partnerships and the balance of Libra. I qualify this general rule by
pointing out that sometimes it does make more sense to see a
house as an inherited energy symbol which is being acted on by a
challenging planet, most often one of the outer, transcendental
planets. Pluto in the Seventh House sometimes can indicate a
need for an individual with too much "Libra-niceness" to inten-
sify and become more powerful in relationships.

While this idea is fairly straightforward, there is a facet of
the theory which needs clarification. Individuals obviously are
going to differ in the extent to which they adapt to the challenge
of a house placement. If a planet positioned in a house is heavily
afflicted, it is probably going to be much more difficult, though
there will simultaneously be more demand, for the individual to
express that area of life successfully than if the planet were
harmoniously aspected. In this sense, there are various degrees of
limitation among house placements. Similarly, the demands for
higher growth in the areas of life related to the house placements
will vary. It is the latter function of a house which rewards

interpretive emphasis, however. Let's consider Saturn as an example. Its house position in the birthchart symbolizes a limitation in the life area that corresponds to that house; at the same time it demands reality-testing and improvement within that area.

While I am completely unprepared to defend its use on astronomical grounds, I find the Equal House system provides me with the most consistent interpretations from this point of view. I find that any planet approaching a few degrees of the next house cusp, and which will progress into the next house during the individual's lifetime, is best considered to be positioned in that next house, since the cusp is a powerful part of the house. When a retrograde planet is near the cusp of a house, and will retrograde back into the previous house by progression, it is better considered in the earlier house. If a planet in the "gray" area before the next house cusp is in a different sign from that on the cusp, I tend to link the planet with the previous house. Finally, if a borderline planet is conjunct a planet deeper into the previous house, I believe it is drawn back into the meaning of that house, unless it clearly progresses into the next house. (All "rules" in this book can be tempered by the reader's sensitivity to as many factors as possible. The ultimate criterion for the interpretation of any factor in the horoscope is the "coherence" or "fit" it makes with the major themes in the chart.)

3

Individual Factors in the Birthchart

Although in this chapter individual astrological factors are discussed separately to highlight their specific contribution to horoscopic analysis, remember that actual practice requires a continual process of synthesis. After all, we're looking for a comprehensive theme that takes all the factors into account in some way. We may need to re-appraise each factor and revise our interpretation several times; our minds must learn to flex their "synthetic muscles" constantly. This point will be made more obvious and substantial when examples of this process will be given. This synthetic process also takes time. It still takes me a couple of separate, intense study periods to really perceive a comprehensive "karmic portrait" of an individual.

A welcome byproduct of this approach is that no specific interpretations need, nor indeed can, be given for any astrological symbol. The meaning of a symbol is hopelessly hypothetical until you know its place in the fabric of the entire chart. The true meaning of Mars in Virgo can only be discerned through its contribution to a general theme in an individual's chart. Whether it manifests primarily as a super-critical "fussbudget" or a consummate craftsperson depends upon its role in the karmic theme of the birthchart.

Some might argue that a symbol actually implies all the possible manifestations consistent with its delineation and that individuals express many of them as the circumstances of life call for them. Although there is some truth here, I feel that this idea encourages the "shotgun" type of reading wherein the astrologer tries to cover every possible meaning of the symbols. This reflects a lack of perspective and little sense of priorities, and does not give clients a clear understanding of their particular situations. There is always an interpretation of a symbol that is most valuable to a client—and that is the one that contributes to the overall theme of the chart. Clients who are presented with a barrage of detail and interpretive "side dishes" remember little of what they have been told.

We may be able to observe behaviors and qualities that correspond to the prominent signs in a person's chart, but without knowing how these qualities relate to the developmental axis, we cannot be of much help to the individual. Many of us highly value, and indeed desperately cling to, qualities that are part of our karmic inheritances. Naturally, we feel more comfortable staying within the familiarity of past-developed territory and following the line of least resistance. Exercising qualities that represent our life-challenges, while ultimately more productive, would be much more disturbing because this would generate the "heat" of resisted change.

Moon's Nodes

I consider this axis to be an important key to the interpretation of a birthchart. Martin Schulman has done some fine work on this factor and on the idea of development from one end of a polar axis to another.[1] It took me a long time to realize, however, that, while the North Node sign and house position are almost always challenges (once in a while I am not sure), the South Node sign and house position are not always inheritances. Indeed, they may be challenges as well. Not understanding this did not invalidate my readings, but some of them were off a bit. It is quite easy to justify a sign as an inheritance when it is really a challenge, due to the power of each zodiacal axis in our lives. When a sign is a major inheritance in a chart, the opposite sign is frequently a major challenge. Both are usually active in our lives and, if we are not careful, we can reverse their roles on the axis.

In the straightforward situation where the South Node is a symbol of inheritance, its energy is expressed with a certain ease. You may be good at something related to this energy. You may make this quality a part of your career or distinguish yourself in some way through the use of it. Let us say that you have the South Node in Capricorn. The world of business or organizational politics may feel very familiar. You may be naturally "down-to-earth" and "in control." Indeed, you may be so much in control of yourself and everyone around you that you have difficulty in interpersonal relationships which require relaxation, vulnerability, and emotional sympathy. In this case, the compulsive nature of the South Node is expressed as rigidity. Transforming the energy is going to be a major challenge in this lifetime.

It is not too difficult to imagine the implied meaning of the North Node within this approach. It is part of the compensatory life-challenge of your present lifetime, and its energy at the other end of the Nodal axis will help draw you out of the rut that the

---

[1]Martin Schulman, *Karmic Astrology: The Moon's Nodes and Reincarnation* (York Beach, Maine: Samuel Weiser, 1975). There is also a gem of a section on the karmic implications of each Nodal axis in *The Astrology of Transcendence*, by Philip Sedgwick (Birmingham, Mississippi: Seek-It Publications, 1980), pp. 45–54.

South Node can represent. It is a dynamic thrust toward balance, an alternative to the stagnation or regression of the South Node. It is a relatively "new" energy, and adjusting to it is likely to be more difficult. You may fear the loss of face implied in having to express yourself in a way with which you are not familiar.

With your South Node in Capricorn you are being challenged to develop Cancerian energy. You need to learn to be softer, more vulnerable, more nurturing, more domestic. These kinds of behaviors are not easy for you; you are afraid you may look silly and anxious if you try them. You may attempt to avoid situations that require these traits, but, because there is a higher, loving wisdom to life, you will be presented with circumstances that demand these responses as challenges to growth.

Saturn

This planet is always a significant factor in the major theme of the chart. As the symbol of boundary and form in life, Saturn's positive, challenging side describes your orientation to the "real" world, your rational plans and goals, your work or level of functional achievement, and how you feel about exerting your will and effort. One of Saturn's roles is to defend and preserve the integrity of your life structures. It can over-react, however, to threats with such negative qualities as contraction, inhibition, fear, rigidity. Saturn, therefore, is an indicator of the limitations of your inheritance.

In my experience, all the combinations of inheritance and challenge are possible with this factor. For example, both the sign and house placements of Saturn could contribute to the inheritance; or both could contribute to the challenge. It seems that frequently Saturn's sign position is at one end of the axis and its house placement is at the other. They rarely are one of the neutral factors in the middle of the axis.

Moon

For our purposes, this luminary's important function is as the adaptive aspect of the ego. It serves as an instinctive, emotional mechanism, enabling the individual to adjust to the environment. Operating subconsciously, it is an "automatic pilot" for activities which neither require, nor allow time for, conscious deliberation. As a storehouse for past experience, the Moon informs us of our needs for emotional survival and security. It is the handmaiden of the Sun, freeing the latter to pursue the goals of the conscious will.

Usually, the Moon represents the inheritance of the past. As you journey along your path, the Moon registers the emotional meaning of your experience. Its very ability to adapt to change provides you with a feeling of stability and security. Karmically, it is usually a clue to where you have been. You are "coming from" the energy symbolized by the Moon sign. The Moon "summarizes" your karmic past and implies an imbalance which will be challenged (depending upon the intensity of its aspects) by other factors. Sometimes, however, the characteristics signified by the Moon's placement in the chart have been introduced in the relatively recent karmic past as an initial thrust toward a challenge; that challenge will be reinforced in this lifetime by other factors in the chart.

One of the reasons the Moon is such a powerful symbol in a horoscope is because its energy operates just below the surface of consciousness and is, therefore, difficult to modify intentionally. Also, the Moon is associated with everyday, mundane activity and describes a continuous experience of ourselves.

. . .

The three factors we have already considered—the South Node, Saturn, and the Moon—constitute a basic complex which can summarize an individual's past karma. Let's imagine that you have the South Node in Aquarius, Saturn in Gemini, and Moon in Virgo. This gives me a tremendous amount of karmic information. A synthesis of these energies reveals a mental orientation, emotional coolness, and a tendency to be aloof and critical in relationships. In addition, you would have the ability to analyze, synthesize, and gain insight through new information. This is a quick summary of your karmic inheritance. We now can begin looking to other factors which will elaborate upon this theme and will signify compensation for this airy emphasis. Possibly your challenge will be toward increased sensitivity (water energy) or warmth (fire energy) to rebalance you.

Because of the airy nature of the other two factors I would approach the interpretation of the Moon in Virgo, in this example, with emphasis on the mental characteristics of the sign. I would not necessarily expect you to be a hard physical worker, as might be true of another person with Moon in Virgo, nor would I expect you to be quite so practical as someone who has an earthy Saturn or Node. This serves as an introduction to the kind of synthesis we will develop as more factors are involved.

Sun

This luminary is unique in its placement along our karmic continuum. It is the most "present-oriented" energy of all the horoscopic factors. The Sun is the facet of the ego which represents creative self-expression. The central factor in the chart, it integrates the other energies into a purpose or direction. It is the mechanism of will, and the sign in which it is placed describes an important synthetic focal point of the conscious personality. It represents a bridge between the past and the future.

When you unlock the creative potential of your Sun sign you experience a sense of cohesion in your life and the feeling of "being yourself." While there is definitely a sense of challenge here, the positive and negative qualities of the Sun sign are typically very explicit in their expression and will permeate the current lifetime. If the potential of the Sun is realized, progress definitely will be made toward rebalancing zodiacal energies.

Mercury and Venus

These planets are being considered together because their range of movement is delimited by their proximity to the Sun. In my experience, they can align themselves together on either, or separately on each, side of the Sun on the karmic continuum. Typically they play a subsidiary role in the fulfillment of the Sun's purposes.

Mercury's sign indicates your mental style. It describes the way you gather and disperse information. It signifies what "wavelength" you are on when you communicate with others. Mercury is associated with the practical, objective functions of mind, the "computer" aspect of the ego. Mercury's placement also describes your nervous system: Mercury in Gemini is high-strung and quick; Mercury in Taurus is more lethargic and slow.

Venus describes your desire for relationship. It wants social and aesthetic harmony. Venus' sign indicates how you give or respond to affection. It suggests what you appreciate or find pleasure in—your emotionally-toned tastes or values. Feminine and receptive, Venus shows how you are likely to use your resources, both psychological (abilities) and physical (money), in the pursuit of pleasure.

Mars

This planet is also supportive of the Sun and its purposes. Like Mercury and Venus, it can place itself on either side of the Sun on the karmic continuum. Mars represents the desire aspect of the ego. It is a symbol of the sexual impulse, aggression, and the method of gratifying ambition. It is a masculine, outward-thrusting force which provides the energy to overcome obstacles to growth and satisfaction.

Jupiter

Like the North Node this planet implicitly falls on the right side of the karmic axis. Jupiter is a strong force for growth. It represents the dynamic aspect of Universal Law—karmic imbalance is compensated for by the urge to expand in the opposite direction. Jupiter is not simply a "benefic." It does not guarantee happiness or prosperity. Rather, it provides an original stimulus toward development according to the style of the sign in which it is located. While it may not be a "new" energy, if there are no other planets in the sign, Jupiter will challenge the individual to transmute the energy into a higher level of expression.

. . .

Unlike the planets we have considered up to this point, which represent various aspects *of* the ego, these bodies represent energies acting *upon* the ego. Their function is to stimulate development toward spiritual balance, but they demand that you transcend the ego rather than merely exercise it. Because these planets move very slowly, their house positions and the aspects they form with the personal planets are extremely powerful agents of change. Their energies are difficult to deal with in a balanced way, however, and can manifest at either end of the inheritance-challenge axis.

Uranus

This planet symbolizes higher mental insights into the workings of the universe. Its energy is expressed with the immediacy of intuition. At a lesser level, it brings about sudden changes as challenges to the rigidity of the ego. Uranus changes and breaks up structures, traditions, and the limitations of time and space, and opens the way for new approaches to reality. It stimulates progressive vision in large groups of people or in society in general, thus producing a widespread increase in consciousness.

Neptune

This planet challenges us to transcend the ego. It simply melts away our defensive structures by giving us a feeling of Unity with all Reality. Neptune challenges us to surrender our separateness and devote ourselves to serving humanity. If we are not responding to Neptune at this mystical level, the planet's energy can manifest as confusion, passivity, and escapism. Or, we might express a less exalted feeling for our fellow beings by being sentimental, indiscriminate, and easily influenced. Neptune can signify sensitivity and vulnerability which enable us to be helpful to others, but if we open ourselves to this energy prematurely we may be frightened by the extreme sensitivity and vulnerability we experience. A healthy respect for the power of these outer planets is necessary.

Pluto

The power of this planet is expressed through destruction and regeneration. An old form dies and a new one is born out of the residue. Ultimately, this applies to the ego itself. Before something new can be built, however, the depths of our being must be plumbed, the hidden material exposed, and a higher integration of the material reached. If we resist this process we may experience violent eruptions — some of which are negatively destructive — as unconscious material is forced to the surface. If we are wedded to our desire egos, Pluto can take the form of secretiveness and manipulation. If we are in the pursuit of truth, we might utilize Pluto's energy in detective work or to understand occult laws. In relationships, Pluto's power can be harnessed in tantric union, dissolving the separativeness of two individuals into a mutual feeling of oneness. The action of this outermost planet is more subtle than Uranus' and more thoroughgoing than Neptune's. All are forms of cosmic grace, and their dynamic thrust is toward the profound realization of all the zodiacal energies.

Part of Fortune

This point, derived from a mathematical relationship among the Sun, Moon, and Ascendant factors, seems to add to our understanding of the individual's karmic situation. Its contribution, however, does not seem to fall consistently on one side or the other of the developmental axis. Like the South Node, its house placement does not seem to follow the rule of indicating a future challenge; sometimes the Part of Fortune represents a past inheritance. Perhaps the safest thing that can be said is that it will reflect and confirm the important themes of the chart, but must be interpreted in the context of the other chart factors.

Midheaven

While I use the Equal House system, I have retained this factor in the chart. Its sign and Sabian Symbol typically contribute to the life-challenge. I support its conventional meaning as one's style of functioning in the world: the way we gain recognition from society.

Ascendant

This point in the chart shows an energy that an individual is "taking on" as a new development. The Ascendant represents a challenge and, therefore, is placed on the right side of the karmic axis. As the cusp of the First House, it suggests a new identity toward which the individual is moving. It describes a "rebirth" of the quality of the sign that is "rising" at the moment of birth. I believe that its traditional reputation as a persona, or face to the world, is consistent with this notion. It often can be seen in the individual's physical or personal appearance because very few people have deeply integrated their Ascendant energy.

Retrogradation

In my experience, this phenomenon has more to do with the sign a planet is in than a quality of the planet's expression. Retrogradation indicates a repetition of the sign's lesson, like another take in the movie-making process. Therefore, it is best interpreted as a challenge, perhaps one that was introduced in the recent karmic past, but which requires more exposure before it can be integrated.

Aspects

This section, as with those on the other astrological factors, does not present full or detailed descriptions of individual aspects. I have no quarrel with the existence of the generally accepted aspects, their orbs of influence or, despite some difference in perspective, their general meanings. I would like to make some broad comments which describe this perspective toward planetary aspects, and which are logical extensions of the approach introduced here.

Most important is my belief that a dynamic interpretation must be made of these factors. Aspects have a purposive dimension as well as a consequential one. (I do not mean to diminish this latter quality of aspects. Many of the "harder" aspects in a chart are valuable as indications of the karmic inheritance, and will be consistent with the other relevant factors.) It is helpful to think of them as serving a developmental function which may have negative karmic implications, but only in an indirect way. In general, I criticize the same "flat" interpretations that I have been criticizing relative to all the astrological factors.

I believe all aspects are demands for transformation and, since I subscribe to the traditional idea of planetary protocol (the faster planet more significantly adapts itself to the slower planet), the demand is for a higher expression of the function of the faster planet. The different types of aspects are simply gradations of intensity of the demand being made. Fundamentally, all the typical negative manifestations of the "harder" aspects are failures to respond constructively to the challenge. They are the residue of resistance to growth.

Let's imagine that you have Mars square Pluto. A traditional interpretation might emphasize that you can be dangerously aggressive, self-defeating, manipulative, sexually perverse, etc. Indeed, these are possible reflections of such an aspect. However, it is also possible that your past karmic inheritance includes a lack of a sense of identity, ambition, or intensity and that you have received this aspect in order to stimulate the milder forms of these aforementioned qualities (assertiveness, courage, the ability to satisfy needs, etc.) for your spiritual advancement. This is a different kind of interpretation, and I can only judge its appropriateness if I know the general theme of the chart and the work you have done in transforming (Pluto) your identity (Mars). If your obvious past karma involves violence and the abuse of power and the chart contains challenge-oriented factors which call for cooperation and service, the aspect usually will reflect a more negative expression requiring self-control and transformation. My point is that the most helpful interpretation could place itself anywhere along this continuum, and must be considered relative to its place in the horoscope as a whole.

I have found that conjunctions, particularly those involving an outer and an inner planet, almost always suggest a challenge rather than an ingrained characteristic. Thus, Neptune conjunct Moon usually seems to indicate that the Moon's energy needs to be refined, transcended, or "melted." Especially in the early part of life, this conjunction may express as confused emotions, extreme vulnerability, and idealization of female relationships;

however, it is important to realize that as the person matures and becomes open to these energies, they can be blended in a higher and more productive way. Again, this is much different from assuming that a person *has* idealized women in the past, or *has* inherited karma as an alcoholic or drug addict! The individual needs to understand the urges to be sensitive to mystical feelings, to sacrifice dependency for the sake of spiritual progress. The negative side of this conjunction only results from resistance.

This theory of interpreting conjunctions seems consistent with the notion that they represent the beginning of a new cycle, much as a New Moon Phase does. Another example may be helpful. A person who has Mars conjunct Saturn in Gemini perhaps is being challenged to learn to discipline and focus mental energy, which may have been scattered in past lives. In this lifetime, this individual is transforming the Gemini energy by going deeper into subjects of study rather than being an intellectual dilettante. How different this interpretation is from one which assumes past karma of frustrated assertiveness.

I do not believe that a trine always implies successful past experiences which created energies that have been carried over to the present. Our gifts and fortunate life events, as well as the totality of our experience and being, are forms of divine expression and serve the purpose of our evolution in consciousness. A trine can serve as a mild form of challenge, urging us to express the qualities involved. However, we can fail to respond to the challenges of trines and waste our energy and talent in degenerate activity. Most of my comments about trines apply to sextiles as well, except that I believe the latter are more challenging and require more conscious effort to manifest.

The only difference I can see between a conjunction and an opposition is that the latter seems to express itself through relationships. In other words, we probably work out the challenge of a conjunction internally, but we need relationships in order to increase our consciousness when an opposition is present. This is particularly true when an outer planet and a personal planet are involved in the aspect. I believe both the conjunction and the opposition represent a challenge to express the energy of the personal planet at a higher level.

The relationship between the Sun and Moon (Lunation Phase)[2] is a particularly important natal aspect and is valuable in understanding an individual's karmic situation. When an aspect is treated as a phase, it is unnecessary to place this factor on one end or other of the developmental continuum. It seems to represent, rather, a synthesis of past and future in one symbol. For example, if your chart contains a Last Quarter Moon Phase, you may have a karmic inheritance of impractical idealism, or an ungrounded spiritual interest. This phase calls for you to make your principles manifest in the real world, to move closer to a practical expression of your vision. For individuals who have relationship problems (shown elsewhere in their charts), a Full Moon Phase may represent a challenge to become more objective about their own egoic positions and learn to cooperate with others. There is a simultaneous expression of inheritance and challenge (based on an implied deficiency that is being remedied) in this factor. I am currently looking at all aspects in this same light, attempting to understand the "phase" in relation to the inheritance-challenge concept.

Sabian Symbols

Several authors have delineated the specific symbolic meaning of each degree of the zodiac. In my opinion the most consistently

---

[2]See Dane Rudhyar, *The Lunation Cycle* (Sante Fe, New Mexico: Aurora Press, 1967).

helpful book on the subject is *The Sabian Symbols in Astrology*, by Marc Edmund Jones.[3] The interpretations were originally rendered by a clairvoyant who visualized pictures for each degree. Jones, presumably, then wrote a prose description of her visions.

When used sensitively, I have found this tool to be invaluable in confirming (in some cases even discovering, though this is more difficult) the inheritance-challenge axis in the chart. Any factor past the exact zero-minute point of a degree is considered as the next degree. These are best considered as challenges; however, the "negative" expressions Jones describes are sometimes startlingly descriptive of inheritances. I go from factor to factor in the chart (omitting the extremely time-sensitive points such as Ascendant, Midheaven, Part of Fortune, etc., in case the birth time is wrong), reading the interpretation given for the degree in which each is placed, while keeping the theme I am currently entertaining in my mind. Usually, it is confirmed, but, occasionally, a totally new direction is discovered.

I also read the description of the degree opposite the one in which each factor is positioned. It seems that the entire axis is operative and the opposite-degree meanings frequently add further clarification of the polarity implied in the inheritance-challenge dimension.

I cannot over-emphasize how important this process has been in validating the interpretations I originally got by other means. I would no longer consider an analysis of a chart complete until it agrees with the descriptions of the Sabian Symbols for each degree.

---

[3]Marc Edmund Jones, *The Sabian Symbols in Astrology* (Stanwood, Washington: Sabian Publishing Society, 1976).

New Moons

This technique is suggested in the pamphlet *The Lunation Process in Astrological Guidance*, by Leyla Rael.[4] It involves taking the Sabian Symbol of the sign and degree of the New Moon which immediately preceded the birth and the two or three which immediately followed (depending upon how old the individual would have been at the last event). It has become obvious to me that these factors give comprehensive summaries of the karmic themes and add emphasis to the information in the rest of the chart.

Miscellaneous Factors

Some traditional procedures of astrological analysis can be adapted to this approach. For example, the zodiac can be divided into personal (Aries, Taurus, Gemini, Cancer), social (Leo, Virgo, Libra, Scorpio), and universal (Sagittarius, Capricorn, Aquarius, Pisces) signs.[5] I feel this is a valid classification system. The personal group deals with personality and the ability to satisfy our own needs, the social signs are concerned with the expression of this personality in social settings and learning to consider the needs of others in one-to-one relationships, and the universal group involves our relationship to larger social groups and the integration of ego-transcending energies. We can tell by looking at which planets are positioned in each category what an individual's past karmic emphasis has been. For example, a person who has certain planets contributing to the inheritance in

---

[4]This pamphlet has been reprinted as part of *The Lunation Cycle*, by Dane Rudhyar (Santa Fe, New Mexico: Aurora Press, 1967).

[5]I would like to give credit for this idea to Richard Idemon.

personal signs may display self-centeredness, have a narrow outlook, and lack objectivity.

We also can observe which planets are placed in personal
(1–4), social (5–8), and universal (9–12) houses. Since I view
houses as compensatory challenges to the energies indicated by
the planets' signs, they represent the emphasis needed to further
growth. I find these two factors to be frequently complemen-
tary. For example, if you have an inheritance of many planets in
personal signs, you are likely to have many of your planets placed
in social or universal houses in order to encourage expansion.

Marc Edmund Jones refined and researched extensively the
importance of the overall chart pattern. I see the pattern as an
indicator of an individual's future challenge. This is obviously
consistent with my idea that the house placements of the planets
are usually demands rather than past tendencies.

Finally, it seems to me that a planet that is very favorably
aspected is usually part of the inheritance, since it is less likely
that a challenging energy would be expressed smoothly.

All the factors in a birthchart can be seen as contributing to
a major developmental theme. While some factors characteristically point to energies we have inherited, and others typically
signify challenges in our lives, the important point is that the
final interpretation only emerges through a holistic perspective.
The general rules applying to the planets, signs, and houses must
be used creatively rather than rigidly. When I first began writing
this book a few years ago, I used these principles routinely.
However, I found there are enough occasions when reversals
occur that tentativeness is always advisable until a full analysis of
the chart is made. Intuition has played more and more of a role in
my work as the years have passed. With this caveat in mind, you
may find figure 3 rewarding as an attempt to summarize these
principles.

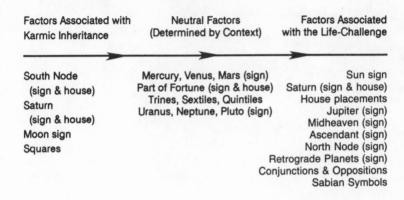

Factors Associated with Karmic Inheritance	Neutral Factors (Determined by Context)	Factors Associated with the Life-Challenge
South Node (sign & house)	Mercury, Venus, Mars (sign)	Sun sign
	Part of Fortune (sign & house)	Saturn (sign & house)
Saturn (sign & house)	Trines, Sextiles, Quintiles	House placements
	Uranus, Neptune, Pluto (sign)	Jupiter (sign)
Moon sign		Midheaven (sign)
Squares		Ascendant (sign)
		North Node (sign)
		Retrograde Planets (sign)
		Conjunctions & Oppositions
		Sabian Symbols

Figure 3. Developmental axis summarizing contribution each astrological factor characteristically makes to overall chart theme.

The factors at the left end of the axis in figure 3 are a core inheritance. They represent qualities that, when positively expressed, are our strongest assets and, when negatively expressed, are our most important limitations. The factors at the right end of the axis demand expansion and change from us. We manifest them clumsily and obsessively for awhile. Only as we mature can we bring gracefulness to their expression.

4

The Zodiacal Signs as Inheritance and Challenge

The zodical signs are the foundation of the inheritance and challenge. As discussed previously, each sign includes a hierarchy of potential expression, from the most primitive to the most sublime levels. The concepts of decanates (each ten-degree division of a sign reflects a sub-theme of each sign of that element) and dwads (each two-and-one-half degree interval of a sign reflects a sub-theme of each of the twelve signs) suggest the infinite shadings possible within each sign. Similarly, their synthesis into an inheritance-group and a challenge-group can manifest at any level.

Some attention to each sign is appropriate in this volume in order to illustrate the point of view I am developing here. While I do not presume to include all the possible themes implied by each sign, I will attempt to present enough themes to give the reader a solid introduction to the type of consideration necessary to eventual syntheses into inheritance- and challenge-groups.

Each sign will be analyzed into broad abstract concepts, from which specific expressions can be inferred by the reader. My belief is that most Sun sign texts over-emphasize the details of each sign at the expense of the general principles involved. Please bear in mind that when I characterize "Aries people" or "Aquarius individuals" a certain way, I know it is simplistic. If you are an Aries Sun or Rising sign, you have other factors modifying its expression. My intention is to consider each sign's nature in a pure form without making it sound so abstract that it can't be applied to the reader's own chart. I will be referring to the higher and lower forms of each sign, which, of course, refer to the negative, unevolved expression of a sign's energy or the more positive, refined qualities of a sign. Inheritance generally indicates the negative qualities while challenge generally refers to the positive.

I have found that the triplicities (elements of fire, air, water, earth), quadruplicities (modalities of cardinal, fixed, mutable), and the individual's orientation to the world (personal, social, universal) provide a foundation for analysis. The polarities of each sign, which correspond to the inheritance and challenge, are readily seen to be the negative and positive expressions of each of these categories. For example, limitations of the sign Aries are arrogance (exaggerated fire), impulsive action (undisciplined cardinality), and selfishness (pure personal energy). On the other hand, a weak individual may be challenged by Aries to be more confident, outgoing, and ambitious.

I will divide each sign into its role in an inheritance-group and challenge-group. The former will take the form of negative qualities in order to cover the range of possible limitations and exaggerations that can contribute to a karmic imbalance. The latter group will consist of positive manifestations of each sign to dramatize the more balanced forms of expression. It is then easy enough to peruse this challenge-group for the positive abilities and talents inherited from past lives. Conversely, the inheritance-group will alert us to the negative ways we may express a challenging energy when we utilize it in a primitive manner.

Aries

Personal—Cardinal—Fire: This sign represents the initial upsurge of individual life; the birth of a separate entity. It is pure self-expression, a raw statement of being, minimally modified by the environment. It expresses itself in a language of survival and manifestation of its essence. Symbolizing the beginning of a cycle, it is the initial thrust of a new direction. Aggression and courage are required so that the individual can break away from the limitations of a past cycle.

Inheritance: This is the first personal fire sign. Aries people can be extremely selfish. They are so busy projecting themselves that they consider others' feelings and opinions to be mere stimuli for their own self-expression. These individuals are protecting the growth of their egos. When Leo and Capricorn also are emphasized, this theme of acquisition for, or expression of, the self can be primary. In my experience, an individual with a primary[1] Aries factor in the inheritance usually has Libra emphasized in the challenge. As with any other zodiacal theme, this challenge can be expressed as planets in Libra, planets in the Seventh House, a Sun-Moon opposition (or other oppositions, for that matter), or Sabian Symbols which demand social cooper-

---

[1]This may be an appropriate place to state a general observation. What more efficient way for nature to remedy an imbalance in one direction than to introduce its opposite as a challenge? One major clue to the chart's karmic theme is the presence of an oppositional axis, although occasionally the opposing signs both can be part of the inheritance or challenge.

ation and egoic restraint. Rounding out a challenge-group in this situation might be Virgo, Libra, Scorpio, Aquarius, and Pisces, all of which can stimulate consideration of another's needs.

Aries is a cardinal sign, and these individuals can be dangerously impulsive. Since they are likely to express the energy in action, they may find themselves making a lot of mistakes and having to learn things the hard way. They rarely test their actions imaginatively beforehand or consider the long-term consequences. They may exaggerate the decisiveness of cardinal action into single-minded obsession, lacking perspective or grace, and distort the leadership potential of the sign into attempts at authoritarian control of others.

An inheritance of impulsiveness and lack of control could combine Aries with Leo, Sagittarius, or possibly lower forms of Gemini, Aquarius, and Pisces. Taurus, Virgo, Libra, Scorpio, and Capricorn would be obvious candidates for a challenge of self-control.

The fire nature of Aries can manifest as an extremely insensitive style of self-expression. Aries energy is so radiant, expansive, and spontaneous that Aries people simply want to do and say whatever comes into their minds. This faithfulness to their inner core of being makes them less attentive to the physical and social environment and sometimes enables them to shortcut a long, painful process of hands-on experience. However, this focus on self-assertion can result in an inability to respond to quiet, deep, subtle experiences.

This energy, when combined with other expansive and expressive signs, such as Gemini, Leo, Sagittarius, and Aquarius, may comprise an inheritance that is insensitive and distant in relationships. Signs such as Cancer, Libra, Scorpio, and Pisces are needed to provide emotional depth and consideration for another's feelings.

Challenge: Since this personal sign naturally looks to its own interests, it can provide individuals in whose charts it is emphasized the courage and strength (though maybe not the persistence) to achieve their goals. Aries is survival-oriented and undaunted by frustration and disappointment. Some individuals have been inundated in the recent karmic past with a great deal of social energy, expressed by signs such as Cancer, Leo, Virgo, Libra, and Scorpio. This can result in a loss of separate identity, and a growing dependence upon others to provide a sense of self-worth. Aries, along with Gemini, Sagittarius, Capricorn, and Aquarius, may be an excellent antidote, and help such individuals regain the uniqueness and independence they need for creative self-expression.

The first cardinal sign, Aries can introduce decisive, creative action into a situation that is bogged down in confusion, passivity, and ineffectiveness. An inheritance that includes signs such as Libra, Sagittarius, Aquarius, or Pisces can suggest a person who is scattered and lazy. Aries can bring single-minded, goal-oriented behavior as a challenge.

An individual may come into the world with a poor self-image and low enthusiasm for life. An inheritance including Virgo, Libra, and Pisces could use Aries as a challenge to give this individual confidence, renewed hope, and a passion for life. The fire element can heat up a cold, unloving emotional nature. A person whose inheritance contains signs such as Gemini, Virgo, Capricorn, and Aquarius might be quite distant and overly rational. Aries, as well as the other fire signs, sometimes brings such people some warm, expansive energy.

At its highest levels of expression, Aries has the capacity to be tremendously creative. There is an ideational quality to Arien creativity; Aries people have no interest in learning from someone else or following conventional lines of thought. As the symbol for birth, Aries represents creativity in a primary form. Action-oriented, it suggests courage, initiative, and, often, leadership potential.

Taurus

Personal — Fixed — Earth: This sign represents the acquisition of resources necessary to sustain the existence of the newly born individual. These resources range from purely material — possessions and money — to a deeper psychological one such as the cultivation of talents which results in a feeling of self-worth. Taurus also is concerned with satisfying physical needs, contentment, and simple sensual pleasures like touching, eating, and moving. Most important to the sign is security, and Taurus uses its stability, determination, and consistency to provide it.

Inheritance: This first personal earth sign can be so obsessed with security that its focus is extremely narrow. Individuals with this energy prominent in their inheritances are so concerned with building their private fortress against loss that they haven't any capacity for broad human perspective. They are so busy buttressing their self-esteem, nursing their talents and abilities, saving their money, and fearfully holding onto their possessions that they deprive themselves of the happiness and sanity which can result from serving others and being more "philosophical" about survival matters. When combined in an inheritance that includes signs such as Aries, Cancer, Leo, lower Scorpio, and Capricorn, this self-obsessed tendency can become a strategy that involves manipulating others in interpersonal relationships and searching for political control. An appropriate challenge in this situation is likely to include signs such as higher Leo, Libra, Sagittarius, and Pisces to encourage a more generous disposition, and signs like Gemini, higher Scorpio, and Aquarius to broaden the mental perspective.

The fixed nature of Taurus is exaggerated as inflexibility, stubbornness, and the kind of narrow-mindedness that is expressed as chauvinism and bigotry. This phenomenon stems from excessive insecurity about one's position. Such people's spirits become petrified in order to preserve the gains they have made. Sometimes, however, to hold on to assets, they must adapt to changing circumstances. In these cases, Taurus gets stuck in a rut, misses opportunities, and actually can lose ground due to over-conservatism. This is most likely when Taurus is combined in the inheritance with lower Cancer, Virgo, lower Scorpio, and Capricorn. Signs such as Aries, Gemini, Sagittarius, and Aquarius can provide the visionary expansion necessary to challenge this tendency.

This first earth sign can be extremely selfish and greedy with regard to material possessions. The security drive can be exaggerated to the point of being obsessed with acquiring and protecting more and more goods. When Taurus is combined with Scorpio and Capricorn, career success and power in the world become too important, requiring a challenge made up of less worldly signs like Aquarius and Pisces.

Excessive earthiness can also manifest as an overly literal, practical perspective with little capacity for subtlety, depth, or imagination. A matter-of-fact attitude may be useful in everyday business matters, but needs to be modified in interpersonal relations and metaphysical seeking. This lower-minded quality can be shared by Gemini, Virgo, and Capricorn.[2]

Taurus can be involved in an inheritance-group which has self-indulgence as its theme. The sensuality and love of pleasure characteristic of this earth sign might be combined with Aries'

---

[2]Again, I would like to remind the reader that I am not attempting to be exhaustive here, but rather to stimulate the lines of thought necessary for the kind of synthesis required by this approach.

impulsiveness, Leo's enthusiasm for entertainment and romance, Libra's desire for a partner, Scorpio's impulse to sexual union, Sagittarius' quest for new forms of stimulation, and Pisces' escapism. Obviously, signs such as Virgo and Capricorn serve to keep this pattern somewhat in line.

Challenge: I frequently have seen Taurus, as part of a challenge, represent attention to self-development. It can stimulate a person to build self-worth through cultivating psychological resources and talents as the basis for self-expression. We can become imbalanced in the direction of social responsibilities to the extent that we lose confidence in our personal foundations. Persons whose inheritance-groups consist of signs like lower Cancer, Virgo, Libra, and Pisces may serve others' needs successfully, yet experience crisis when left on their own. In this situation, Aries, Leo, and Capricorn would stimulate qualities such as personal ambition, the need for security, and achievement through productive effort.

As a steadying, peaceful energy, the higher forms of this fixed sign can bring relief to an individual who has been through a period of emotional turbulence and stress. (This could show up as an inheritance-group containing the lower forms of the water signs, along with Sagittarius and Aquarius.) When combined with the ground-rock of higher Leo, or the transcendent flow of higher Pisces, an individual's challenge can represent a comforting, refreshing balance to the chaos of preceding cycles.

Similarly, a person could have inherited complex karma, stemming from a previous cycle that emphasized higher universal truths (Sagittarius, Aquarius), psychic manipulations (Scorpio, Pisces), or higher career considerations (Capricorn). This person has lost the ability to "smell the roses." Taurus can spearhead a challenge toward simplicity, groundedness, and sensual innocence as a compensatory direction. Along with Taurus, signs like

Aries, Gemini, and Cancer can contribute to the "back to basics" nature of this challenge.

Gemini

Personal — Mutable — Air: The individual now reaches out to the nearby environment to exchange information which is crucial for practical adaptation and increased growth. Gemini represents the ability to make associations and synthesize pieces of information for maximum usefulness. Gemini is also the sign of superficial contacts that bring us into everyday commerce as an initial participation in our culture.

Inheritance: This is the first personal air sign. Its concerns are so local, so vital to our ideas of personal expansion, that we can be petty, superficial, and fickle. This self-centered quality of Gemini's thinking and communication can be exaggerated to the extent that the concerns of everyday commerce dominate our relationships. Gemini is a practical mentality, searching for knowledge that expands the ego and provides a broader foundation for personal security. These worries and concerns can prove boring and annoying to people with broader perspectives.

When these qualities are combined in an inheritance with signs such as Taurus, Virgo, or Capricorn, the theme can become one of narrowness of perspective, concern only with the mundane, and materialistic obsession. A challenge to this imbalance might consist of signs such as Cancer, Scorpio, Sagittarius, Aquarius, and Pisces. These would deepen and broaden the individual's orientation to life.

Negatively, Gemini's mutability may show up as amorality, indecisiveness, skepticism, instability, lack of focus, and irresponsibility. When Gemini is combined in the inheritance with signs such as Aries, Libra, Sagittarius, Aquarius, and Pisces, this lack of a firm position can be a major chart theme. Energies such as Taurus, Virgo, Scorpio, and Capricorn can provide an antidote of stability and strength of purpose.

A karmic limitation of this air sign is mental defensiveness which causes the individual to be conniving, emotionally cold, callously insensitive, and verbally caustic. With signs such as Virgo, Libra, Capricorn, and Aquarius, a broader theme of inter-personal distance and emotional repression can be formed. The challenge-group might consist of warm signs such as Aries, Leo, or Sagittarius to increase spontaneity, or the water signs, to temper intellect with feeling.

Sociability is another quality of the air signs. Gemini can be promiscuous, shallow, uncommitted, and deceitful (as can Aries, Sagittarius, Aquarius, and Pisces). Social stability is more charac-teristic of Cancer, Virgo, Scorpio, and Capricorn.

Challenge: This personal sign provides us with the contacts and information we need to prosper as growing organisms. It acts like an antenna, alert to whatever will ensure security and safe ego-expansion. While there can be an abstract quality to its action, it is pragmatic enough to provide grounding in the ele-mentary social interactions and commerce of the culture, when combined with Taurus, Cancer, Virgo, and Capricorn. This combination can be a challenge to an inheritance that represents a loss of connection to ordinary life, or an overly dramatic or unworldly karma (suggested by signs such as Scorpio, Sagittar-ius, Aquarius, or Pisces).

Gemini's adaptability allows us to get along with a diverse selection of people; thus, Gemini people are often popular. The sign is people-oriented, friendly, charming, and witty. Other socially oriented signs are Leo and Libra. These might counter the isolationist tendency of an inheritance such as Aries or Pisces.

Since Gemini has no need for commitment or deep intimacy, this energy can contribute to an independent and freedom-loving orientation. It is versatile and open-minded, pursuing a wide range of ideas to stay informed. Along with Aries, Libra, higher Scorpio, Sagittarius, Aquarius, and Pisces, it can form a challenge to an individual who has gotten stuck in a rigid, unadaptive, narrow-minded, emotionally dependent position (which can happen to signs such as Taurus, Cancer, Virgo, lower Scorpio, and Capricorn).

Rather like a computer, Gemini's lower mind stores, associates, and creatively synthesizes new data to efficiently negotiate day-to-day activities. Because it is unemotional, it can contribute rationality to the decision-making process. A curious sign, it stimulates a desire for new data. Signs such as Taurus, Cancer, Leo, and Capricorn can become stultifyingly contented with their lot. Gemini, along with Aries, Libra, Scorpio, Sagittarius, Aquarius, and Pisces can form a challenge to this tendency.

Gemini can be a breezy, light, playful breath of fresh air in a life that has become bogged down by heaviness and suffering. A blithe spirit, it can refresh an individual who has been excessively imbalanced toward work or a higher search for meaning.

Cancer

Personal — Cardinal — Water: Cancer represents the instinct to build a solid emotional foundation as a basis for further growth. The goal is to establish roots in an intimate social arrangement, to be part of a "family." This satisfies the need for security and enables the individual to expand to wider and deeper forms of self-expression. The emotional depth inherent in this stage provides necessary training for other intense relationships to come. Qualities to be learned here are vulnerability, appreciation for the domestic environment, and nurturance.

Inheritance: An imbalance in this personal water sign can manifest as an extremely insecure emotional foundation, which may be expressed as childish dependency, selfish neediness, and helpless ineffectuality. Individuals who fail to complete the stage (where they need to be taken care of) may go through their lives viewing everyone else as "parents." Cancer in the inheritance can manifest as a person who is afraid to stray far from the domestic nest and interact with the outer world.

Like all water signs, Cancer can be moody, hyper-sensitive, and defensively withdrawn. People with this most fundamentally vulnerable energy in the inheritance probably experience more pain than others from deprivation or rejection. This particular tendency can be countered by a challenge that includes the emotional distance of air signs or the buoyancy of fire signs.

Persons with Cancer in their inheritance can share their feelings of emotional dependency with others whose charts contain water signs, as well as Leo and Libra. The more detached signs — Aries, Gemini, Sagittarius, Capricorn, and Aquarius — counterbalance Cancer's emotionalism. Cancer's unwillingness to face the world and its practical demands is, again, a water-sign liability, sometimes shared by Libra and Sagittarius. The earth signs provide a most effective antidote for this karmic inheritance.

Negative cardinal behavior characteristic of Cancer could be nagging, manipulation, greediness, or smothering over-protectiveness. This inheritance may also be combined with the demanding qualities of Taurus, Leo, and lower Scorpio. An individual with this inheritance would need to become more self-sustaining and mature in relationships with others, more capable of equal give-and-take. This might be accomplished through a challenge-group which includes Libra, higher Scorpio, Capricorn, Aquarius, and Pisces.

Challenge: Sometimes we become involved too much in outer, worldly affairs, focusing on our careers, politics, social change, etc. Perhaps we have a lot of Capricorn or Aquarius energy in our charts. An imbalance may develop whereby we lose an appreciation for home and family. We could be so wrapped up in other people's problems, or in material acquisition, that we don't notice that we're not satisfying ourselves or our intimates emotionally. A Cancer challenge can reestablish the importance of a secure emotional base in our lives.

Cancer takes care of emotional "business." It can be protective, nurturing, and helpful. When we are in touch with our deepest emotional needs, we understand the responsibility we have to serve each other. Signs such as Aries, Sagittarius, Capricorn, and Aquarius sometimes lose sight of this and can be guilty of selfish blindness. When Cancer combines with Virgo, Libra, Scorpio, or Pisces, a challenge is formed which can counter excessive detachment.

Emotional depth, sensitivity, and attention to the demands of intimate relationships are the province of water energy. Cancer's emphasis is on awareness of our most basic dependency needs and the need for parental, family, and other domestic relationships. The other water signs combine well with Cancer in a challenge of feeling energy. An individual who has become too sophisticated and complicatedly worldly (whose inheritance includes Sagittarius, Capricorn, and Aquarius) might have Cancer as the challenge united with the other personal signs, indicating a need to return to basics.

Leo

Social—Fixed—Fire: Leo represents the need for creative self-expression. By this stage, the individual has successively established the different separate aspects of selfhood, and now feels a powerful impulse to integrate them in a way that attracts wider social contact and approval. This is an expansive stage, one which implies an excess of being, a capacity to demonstrate some complexity of development. In the Leo stage, we flex our egoic muscles, exercise selfhood, and strive to learn who we are from the results of our efforts or the reactions of others.

Inheritance: People with a Leo inheritance are tremendously interested in social activity, and can become quite dependent on it. Their need for applause after their performances may be compulsive. The tendency is to exaggerate qualities; to be always "on"; to constantly sell their expressive goods. This strategy manifests as superficiality, insincerity, and fickleness in relationships. The social playfulness of Leo can take the form of sexual promiscuity, frivolous self-indulgence, and failure at intimacy. Such individuals are likely to be self-centered and insensitive to the needs of others. When Leo is combined in an inheritance with energies like Aries, Gemini, Sagittarius, or lower Aquarius, relationships can be mutually unsatisfying and short-lived. An antidote could be a challenge consisting of Cancer, Virgo, Scorpio, and Capricorn, signs that understand give-and-take and commitment.

Because the energy of Leo is linked to the ego, people who have this sign in the inheritance try to avoid experiences that do not bolster their confidence. Failure and rejection of any kind are resisted strongly. Leo individuals can be extremely defensive and stubborn in the face of frustration. In order to protect themselves against any such incidents in the future, they can become absurdly rigid and demanding. When Leo is combined with the other fixed signs, or with Virgo or Capricorn, the need for adaptability, flexibility, and humor is paramount. Aries, Gemini, Libra, Sagittarius, and Pisces might be valuable in a challenge-group.

A social fire sign, Leo's optimism and vitality can be exaggerated as arrogance, dramatic abuses of power, and careless expenditure of physical energy. These faults would be reinforced by Aries, Scorpio, and Capricorn in the inheritance. Compensation for this type of imbalance might be offered by less personally ambitious signs such as Taurus, Cancer, Aquarius, or Pisces.

Challenge: Leo stimulates creative self-expression. Karmically, the person who has Leo in the challenge may have become imbalanced in the direction of focusing on issues of broad social import. Through Leo, such people may learn to serve humankind directly or by spreading ideas that can raise the consciousness of individuals. Perhaps the chart is strong in the universal signs (or Libra) and suggests a person who has lost touch with the inner core and sacrificed a certain amount of effective strength. This individual may promote the creative contributions of others or scatter energy in an abstract or impersonal way. Leo, like Aries, can reorient the ego dimension in such a way that the individual becomes more personally grounded.

Leo shares a kind of endurance, a stubborn refusal to be manipulated or easily discouraged from reaching a goal, with signs like Taurus, Scorpio, and Capricorn. A challenge-group containing these signs provides "backbone" to a chart that has an inheritance dominated by mutable signs or easily distracted cardinals like Aries and Libra.

A group of signs containing Gemini, Cancer, Virgo, Libra, and Pisces can form an inheritance that suggests that self-confidence has been undermined. In this situation, Leo seems invariably to be part of a challenge to restore optimism, enthusiasm, and ego strength. Or, it might represent movement from introversion and distance to warmth and sociability. Usually, Leo teams up with Aries and Sagittarius to accomplish this.

Virgo

Social — Mutable — Earth: This sign's purpose is to take the rough-hewn form of the fully developed ego and prepare it for the mutuality and sacrifice of intimate relationships. Improvement, purification, and integration, leading to eventual perfection, are keywords for this process. Every aspect of the being, as well as the environment, needs to be inspected and evaluated for its usefulness toward this goal.

Inheritance: Virgo individuals, when their energy is imbalanced, tend to obsessively identify, and attempt to remedy, imperfections both in themselves and others. Discrimination gets exaggerated into fussiness; analytic ability becomes a psychological "hatchet-job"; self-improvement yields to moral righteousness. The individual is too sharp-edged, judgmental, and intolerant to engage gracefully in interpersonal relations. Gemini, Capricorn, and Aquarius aggravate the situation. Signs such as Cancer, Leo, Libra, Sagittarius, and Pisces can provide compensation by adding warmth and compassion.

The mutable nature of Virgo can be expressed negatively as over-zealous mental vigilance. The egoic "stone" is being polished with an excessively abrasive material. Such perfectionism yields inhibition, self-doubt, anxiety, and servility. Other energies in such an inheritance-group can be Taurus, Capricorn, and Pisces. The antidote for this theme is usually a reinstatement of fire energy, which bolsters self-confidence and energizes self-expression.

As an earth sign, a Virgo individual can pick a lot of nit. Virgo's desire for order and detail can become quite compulsive. Its earthy practicality can manifest as pettiness, narrowness of perspective, and too much attention to routine matters. Signs like Taurus, Gemini, and Capricorn can support this small-minded tendency. The compensatory theme may be toward broadening the perspective through the universal signs (Sagittarius, Aquarius, and Pisces) or deepening the emotional nature through Cancer and Scorpio.

Challenge: Virgo can represent an antidote (along with Cancer, Libra, Scorpio, and Pisces) to an inheritance which suggests that the individual has forgotten how to serve other people. True service simply means action which enhances the real well-being of another. This can be at any level, from making someone a sandwich to providing insight into self-destructive tendencies. People with signs like Aries, Taurus, Leo, Sagittarius, Capricorn, and lower Aquarius in their inheritances can be too wrapped up in their own affairs to be aware of others' needs. Virgo's concern for making things better enables it to see what others need.

Because it requires a certain amount of awareness to accomplish its purposes, Virgo increases an individual's consciousness. It can be grouped with the air signs, or with Scorpio and Sagittarius, as a stimulus to further mental growth. Water signs can become preoccupied with developing deep inner resources, and fire signs with engaging spontaneous self-expression, both at the expense of conceptual understanding. We can sometimes lose our bearings without the discipline of discrimination and rational choice. We can fall into self-indulgence under the guise of "following our instincts."

Personal competence and conscientious discipline in practical affairs are Virgo's specialties. Its natural attunement to detail, cautious consideration, analytical and organizational abilities, all enable it to effectively "take care of business." The capacity to discriminate and see clearly the reality of a situation can provide a challenge to people with an imbalance of Pisces (or Aries, Gemini, Leo, Sagittarius, and Aquarius), who can be blinded by sentiment, egotism, or self-indulgence.

Libra

Social — Cardinal — Air: This sign represents the midpoint between the pure subjectivity of Aries and the total loss of subjectivity at the end of Pisces. Libra is interested in balance, primarily in relationships, between self-satisfaction and attention to another's needs. Libra's focus is cooperation and commitment to lasting unions, such as marriage and other partnerships. This sign also possesses objectivity and detached judgment, such as is required in the pursuit of justice, peace, and true illumination.

Inheritance: The exaggeration of this energy is an excessive need for relationships. These individuals may have difficulty spending any time alone. They may depend too much on partners and their dependency can be stifling. Strongly Libran people may be so insecure and concerned with other people that they lose track of their own goals and directions. This is especially likely if Libran factors are combined with other social signs (Leo, Virgo, Scorpio) or Cancer. This inheritance-group needs to be challenged by more independent signs like Aries, Gemini, Sagittarius, Capricorn, and Aquarius.

A more aggressive form of Libra's problem is its tendency toward superficiality and self-indulgence. Rather than forming committed relationships, these Librans are more interested in partying and endless socializing. The stimulation of new people, the glamor of rising on the social ladder, and sexual flirtation all can become disorienting obsessions. This would be reinforced by an inheritance that contains the other social signs (except Virgo), as well as Gemini. A challenge-group characterized by discrimination and self-control might include Taurus, Virgo, and Capricorn, and can serve as an antidote to this tendency.

Libran individuals sometimes strive so hard for balance that they are incapable of taking any stand; the result is indecision and confusion. The ability to see both sides of an issue and the fear of offending anyone can make them incapable of practical judgment. This can be exacerbated by Gemini and Pisces. A challenge-group consisting of Aries, Leo, Virgo, Scorpio, and Capricorn can counterbalance this by providing strength and clarity of mind.

Challenge: Libra in the challenge-group helps compensate for an imbalance, either toward self-centeredness or toward overly universalized relationships. Perhaps these individuals are preoccupied with establishing the foundations of their own being. Their principle concerns might be accumulating resources to provide security (personal signs). Or, they may be emphasizing career success at the expense of relationships (Aries, Taurus, Scorpio, Capricorn). Libra joined by Cancer, Aquarius, and Pisces could lead these individuals to place more importance on relationships or idealistic values.

Persons who have scattered energy in universal directions might need an impetus to return to relationships that demand more intimacy and commitment. This Libran challenge may be complemented by Virgo, Scorpio, and Capricorn.

A more passive expression of this energy might be an individual who is so inhibited and fearful of being hurt in relationships of any kind that it is debilitating (Taurus, Cancer, Virgo, Scorpio, and Pisces could indicate this). Libra can stimulate the urge to meet people and get involved in relationships. Along with Gemini, Leo, Sagittarius, and Aquarius, this sign can help a person understand the ground-rules for sociability.

Libra helps us achieve balance in our mental perspective and cultivate dispassionate objectivity. It represents the principle of awareness through relationship, gives us feedback from others, and reveals us to ourselves. Libra offers an opportunity for illumination by placing us in the witness position — even relative to ourselves. Along with the other air signs, and Virgo, this perspective can counterbalance an overly subjective or unconsciously instinctual, approach to life (such as would be likely in a person whose chart shows an inheritance of Aries, Taurus, Cancer, Leo).

Scorpio

Social — Fixed — Water: Having learned to appreciate the give-and-take of relationships, Scorpio's ultimate goal is to deepen this capacity and, through the kind of surrender demanded in tantric sexuality, to engage relationship as a vehicle for God-union. The Scorpio person needs to let the ego "die" so that a wider consciousness can be born (thus, the destruction and rebirth aspects of this sign). Scorpio seeks to get to the essence of all matters and purge them of impurities and obstructions to transcendence.

Inheritance: Scorpio can corrupt the urge for intimacy and become exploitive and manipulative. These individuals find obstructions in their partners and attempt to "transform" them, to create pure vessels. Although the goal is ego-transcendence, it becomes perverted into attempts to control other people and the environment totally. When Scorpio is combined with signs such as Aries, Leo, and Capricorn, this need for control and power can form the theme of a karmic inheritance. Sexual obsession and perversion can be other detours along the road to true tantric union. Taurus, Virgo, Sagittarius, and Pisces in the challenge can encourage Scorpios to relax this control mechanism through innocence, humility, faith, and surrender.

Although Scorpio aggressively strives to transform others, it strongly resists any attempts by other people to influence it. Secretive, it does not give any clues about itself; stubborn, it holds onto the most untenable position; paranoid, it attributes problems to other people. Scorpio's inflexibility is shared, of course, by the other fixed signs, and its desire to lead, rather than be led, is common to Aries and Capricorn. The mutable signs, along with Libra, can serve as a challenging antidote to this karmic theme.

Like the other water signs, and Virgo, Scorpio can be excessively sensitive. Reactive emotions of sullen hurt, grudge-holding withdrawal, stinging sarcasm, jealous rage, and ruthless retaliation are characteristic expressions of this liability. Air signs frequently constitute a compensatory challenge, since they encourage emotional distance and objectivity. Taurus might contribute patience and self-control, and Sagittarius might add a philosophical buffer.

Challenge: In order to achieve the desired union, the Scorpio individual must get to know the potential partner. Intimacy requires understanding and profound sensitivity to the other's needs. The union must be emotional and intellectual as well as sexual. This sign represents the intense culmination of the progression of relationship that began at Cancer and developed through Leo, Virgo, and Libra. As a challenge-group, the social signs compensate for an inheritance describing an individual who has difficulty perceiving others' needs (Aries, Taurus, Gemini, Sagittarius).

Scorpio, when combined with the other fixed signs, or Aries and Capricorn, can bolster an individual's emotional fortitude. A mature person must be able to stand firm in the face of trivial fashion, social pressure, and arbitrary cultural standards in order to grow strong and genuine. Signs which seem to require such a challenge are the mutables and Libra. This inheritance, at best flexible and adaptable, can be wobbly and ineffectual.

I have frequently seen Scorpio (along with the other water signs) bring depth and sensitivity to individuals who have become totally immersed in work (earth signs), or in the world of ideas (air signs). In sexual relationships, Scorpio can add passion to an inheritance that otherwise shows a lack of intensity.

Sagittarius

Universal — Mutable — Fire: Having developed the capacity through the social signs for intimacy in one-to-one relationships, Sagittarius now encourages social expansion and the exploration of ideas and values which are important to large groups of people. Through extensive travel and diverse experience, this sign gains insights and understanding that it can apply toward the development of moral and legal guidelines for cultural cohesiveness. The idealism and ethical strength of this sign are part of its "straight-ahead" approach to life, both in action and communication.

Inheritance: Sagittarius is interested in ideal human potentials and expanding the limits of experience and knowledge. Its optimism, however, can reach absurd proportions. Its moral standards, too, can become exaggerated into fanaticism and self-righteousness. This inherited tendency could be exacerbated when combined with Virgo, Scorpio, Capricorn, and Pisces. These people need to learn to appreciate the "everyman" in all of us; Taurus, Cancer, Libra, and Aquarius can help accomplish this.

The mutable nature of Sagittarius can be exaggerated into irresponsibility. Restless and easily bored, Sagittarians want to enjoy freedom and can be quite self-indulgent in their lack of commitment. They love diversity and change, and tend to scatter their energies, rarely applying themselves to long-range goals that require discipline and patience. Their flighty nature makes commitment in relationships difficult. When Sagittarius is combined in an inheritance with Aries, Gemini, Aquarius, and Pisces, there is a need for a challenge which provides stability and persistence. Taurus, Virgo, Scorpio, and Capricorn frequently compose this group.

All the fire signs expand the ego in a characteristic way. When Aries and Leo are part of the inheritance, the individual's straightforward style can become obnoxious "truth-telling," tactless insensitivity, and bombastic self-inflation. Or, feelings of real friendliness can be exaggerated into sugar-coated superficiality. Gemini, Leo, Libra, and Pisces sometimes can participate in such a tendency. A challenge-group of signs that provide a more realistic self-appraisal, such as Taurus, Virgo, Scorpio, Capricorn, and Aquarius, can come to the rescue here.

Challenge: These people want to create the moral foundations of a cooperative society. Philosophical and religious principles are byproducts of expansive intuition and abstract mental processes. These individuals, when inspired, provide the underpinning for our legal and political systems. Cancer and Libra have some interest in these issues, also, but Sagittarius seeks to develop them on a universal scale. This challenge is a compensatory direction for persons who either are limited to personal concerns (Aries, Taurus, Cancer), or who are attempting to satisfy intimate social needs (Leo, Libra, Scorpio) to the exclusion of these higher considerations.

Sagittarius energy provides us with the thrills of expansive and adventurous experience. From the excitement of athletics to the fruits of travel and exploration, this sign rules activity that adds to our understanding of what is possible in this world. It represents the courage necessary for informed evaluation of human limits. Aries, Leo, Scorpio, and Aquarius could support this task. These signs counterbalance an inheritance of ossified personal structures (Taurus, Cancer, Virgo, Capricorn).

Along with the other fire signs, Sagittarius contributes the positive qualities of enthusiasm, buoyancy, happiness, and joie de vivre. We are lifted by this energy and feel extroverted, gregarious, and kind. We have faith in the grace of the greater cosmic order and are able to appreciate the spark of inherent goodness in our fellow beings. Gemini, Libra, and Aquarius would add the values of brotherhood and social cooperation. These qualities challenge an individual who is too fearful or introverted (dominated by the feminine signs of earth and water) to enjoy the more expansive side of life.

Capricorn

Universal — Cardinal — Earth: Sagittarius provides the abstract principles by which a society could function. Capricorn's task is to transform them into rules and disciplines so that they may be applied practically. Capricorn takes the consensus of the members of the social group and organizes the details into laws, institutions, and penalties. This sign also supports steady, orderly attempts toward achievement within the cultural structure.

Inheritance: Capricorn individuals can pay a high price for excessive conformity to the cultural "party line." Caught up in the superficial externals which guarantee success, they may lose sight of their individual *dharma*. In the extreme, they became robotized, suppressing the creative impulses necessary for unique contributions to humanity. Disciplines and "shoulds" influence them and their decisions too strongly. Other earth signs, the cardinals (except for Aries), and Virgo can support such an imbalance. The more creative, individualistic signs, such as Aries, Gemini, Leo, and Aquarius, can serve as a potent challenge-group.

As a sign of leadership, Capricorn can become corrupted by its desire for power and control. Usurping human rights, as is typical of totalitarian governments, is a liability of this energy's influence. If combined in an inheritance with Aries, Leo, and Scorpio, a major theme is evident. Taurus, Cancer, Libra, Aquarius, and Pisces can serve to compensate for this tendency, since they can represent sacrificial service to others.

Like Taurus and Virgo, Capricorn easily can become dry and narrow in its expression. Harried businesspeople whose desperate need to rise in the company leads them to neglect partners and families are classic examples of this limitation. Dullness, rigidity, and a joyless perspective can develop when these signs dominate an inheritance. Cancer, along with almost any of the other non-earth signs, can remedy this imbalance of worldliness and achievement-orientation.

Challenge: Capricorn focuses attention on the value of culture and tradition. A strong social agreement, developed through centuries of experience with basic life-positive values, can be quite important to an individual's development. This is the function of culture. We pass on valuable secrets about life through the wisdom of the past. Cancer, Libra, and Sagittarius seem to be involved in this task. Together with Capricorn, they could make up a counterbalancing influence for an individual who has become eccentrically individualistic and self-centered, whose inheritance might include Aries, Gemini, Leo, and Aquarius.

Capricorn can stimulate the development of responsibility in an individual. Willingness to assume a position of accountable competence is the basic element of leadership. The drive to achieve such a status is one aspect of ambition, another of Capricorn's hallmarks. The desire for power and control are others. As part of such a challenge, we might find Aries, Leo, and Scorpio. These signs would be appropriate compensation for an inheritance that suggests a reluctance to assume leadership, indicated by signs such as lower Cancer, Virgo, Libra, and Pisces.

The earthy side of Capricorn teaches practicality and realism. It instills persistence and steadiness in the pursuit of long-term goals. Capricorn also provides the discipline needed to focus and order energy rather than scattering it in unproductive directions. Taurus, Virgo, and Scorpio can join with it to form a thematic challenge-group. People whose inheritance includes Aries, Gemini, Sagittarius, Aquarius, and Pisces could benefit from such an influence.

Aquarius

Universal—Fixed—Air: The cultural tradition of Capricorn needs to be challenged and refreshed by new creative ideas that will stimulate continued evolution of consciousness. Aquarius, being attuned to the universal mind, revolutionizes our perspective at the appropriate time so that we do not become stagnant and rigid. At all levels it breaks down limitations that form out of inertia and resistance to change. It helps to ensure that the strictures of conventional society do not violate the natural freedoms of the individual.

Inheritance: In its attempts to correct society's ills, Aquarius feels the need to join with others and communicate a message of criticism and redirection. People of this sign can get so caught up with the urgency and grandness of this mission that they ignore simple loving relationships. The "cause" can become more important than the people it is supposed to educate. These individuals become too abstract and idealistic in the heat of carrying out their transforming function. Scattering their energy to reach a wide audience causes them to lose interpersonal perspective. Sagittarius and Pisces may combine with Aquarius to form an inheritance-group along these lines. The antidote is represented by the social lessons of Cancer, Leo, Libra, and Scorpio.

Aquarius carries out its work by resisting conventional dogma. It rebels against whatever fails to adapt to changing times or the needs of all individuals. When exaggerated, this quality can become cantankerous eccentricity, isolated individualism, and revolutionary violence. Aquarius guards against a repressive cultural monstrosity, but can err in the direction of social breakdown and unproductive anarchy. Individualistic tendencies can also be expressed in this inheritance by signs such as Aries, Gemini, and Sagittarius.

The image of the absent-minded professor appropriately describes the liabilities of Aquarius air. These people live too much "in their heads," distracted from the realities of practical and social responsibilities. A karmic inheritance of this nature might also include the other air signs, and possibly Pisces. Earth signs can help people with this inheritance carry out their visions in the "real" world.

Challenge: Aquarius forces us to broaden our perspective and consider what things could be like if we creatively changed them. This sign gives us a kick in our intellectual pants when we get into a rut. Society would become totally predictable and stagnant without Aquarius. This sign usually combines in a challenge-group with Gemini, Scorpio, Sagittarius, and Pisces, whenever rigidity or superficiality dominates an inheritance (possibly consisting of Taurus, Virgo, Libra, and Capricorn).

Aquarius' truth is based on tapping into the universal mind, to which we open ourselves when we're ready. Unlike Gemini and Libra, which are more vulnerable to social influence, Aquarius holds firmly to its opinions regardless of pressure from conventional society. It, therefore, contributes courage and steadfastness to individuals who tend to "waffle" in their beliefs (as can happen with Gemini, Libra, and Pisces). The fixed signs, along with Virgo and Capricorn, can support Aquarius in a challenge-group.

A universal air sign, Aquarius stimulates the kind of creative thinking that has resulted in tremendous scientific advances. We must open our minds to new perspectives on familiar objects and situations in order to find new approaches to problems. Taurus, Cancer, Virgo, Libra, and Capricorn can form an inheritance that is either too habit-bound, literal, conventional, or superficial to lead to creative contributions. A challenge-group consisting of creative energies such as Aries, Leo, Scorpio, and Pisces, along with Aquarius, can serve to counterbalance this limitation.

Pisces

Universal — Mutable — Water: This sign's function is to stimulate the sense of oneness, of interconnectedness, with all individuals and the manifest world. It accomplishes this by transcending physical limits, structures, and concepts. It impels us into the etheric realm where, through the gesture of surrender, we tap into the universal psyche. Out of this general process come self-sacrifice, compassion, sensitivity, and fantasy, characteristics for which this sign is known.

Inheritance: Pisces represents the non-material side of life, and individuals with a strong component of this energy may have difficulty functioning in or showing much interest in the physical world. They may be preoccupied with their inner experiences, too "spacey" and unrealistic to handle practical affairs. If combined in an inheritance-group that includes Libra, Sagittarius, or Aquarius, this can suggest a major karmic theme. Signs which tend to bring the individual into the manifest world—earth signs, Gemini, and Cancer—can compensate for this tendency. Everyday relationships also may be too demanding and ordinary to interest these people. They are interested in more dramatic, "cosmic" things. Along with Sagittarius and Aquarius, individuals with a Pisces inheritance may need to be challenged by signs such as Gemini, Capricorn, and all the social signs in order to remind them of interpersonal responsibilities.

Pisces energy offers wholeness of experience but, when exaggerated, can result in confusion, internal chaos, vagueness, dishonesty, and self-delusion. Lack of stability can be the major theme of an inheritance which also includes Aries, Cancer, Gemini, and Sagittarius. To compensate for this imbalance, a challenge-group of earth signs and the fixed signs could provide inner strength.

A strong Pisces component (along with other water signs in the inheritance) can produce painful vulnerability to the negative vibrations in the world. People with this inheritance may absorb an emotional environment wholesale, but not be able to separate external experiences from those originating in their own psyches.

Such supersensitivity can lead to withdrawal, escapist forms of addiction, and self-destructive martyrdom. A challenge comprised of the masculine signs (especially air) seems to be the most effective balance to this affliction.

Challenge: Frequently I find that a Pisces challenge, along with higher Cancer, Virgo, higher Scorpio, and Aquarius, will stimulate a service-oriented, humanitarian impulse in a person who has been overly self-centered. An inherited imbalance of self-centeredness may be suggested by a group consisting of Aries, Taurus, lower Cancer, Leo, lower Scorpio, and lower Capricorn.

A major karmic theme that I have frequently found is one oriented toward power and control. This tendency would be represented by an inheritance of Aries, Leo, Scorpio, and Capricorn. Such individuals may always be scheming, manipulating, and jockeying for a position in life. They need to learn the value of simplicity, vulnerability, humility, and service to others. Taurus, Cancer, Virgo, and Pisces can help in such cases and enable them to achieve more balance and adaptability.

Pisces is frequently part of a challenge-group which deepens an individual's nature. Perhaps this person has been obsessed with the superficial struggle for material gain (earth), or with mastering problems via the intellect (air). The presence of Pisces always stimulates at least a primitive sense of the more spiritual meaning of life.

5

A Fuller Treatment of Synthesis

We have discussed the general concept of this approach and possible metaphysical implications. We have been introduced to the developmental axis, a polarity of karmic inheritance and life-challenge. We have looked at the ways various astrological factors contribute to this axis. We have considered the zodiacal signs and some possible ways they can combine to form an inheritance or a challenge.

Perhaps some examples would illustrate this process further. In figure 4 on page 66, I have deliberately chosen signs at the ends of the axis that have differing elements within each group in order to introduce some complexity into the process. We will limit ourselves to the signs rather than introduce the specific factors involved.

We want to find some concepts that all three signs have in common. For the inheritance, we want to identify a theme which represents a negative adaptation. How might Aries, Scorpio, and Capricorn express themselves in a common, negative

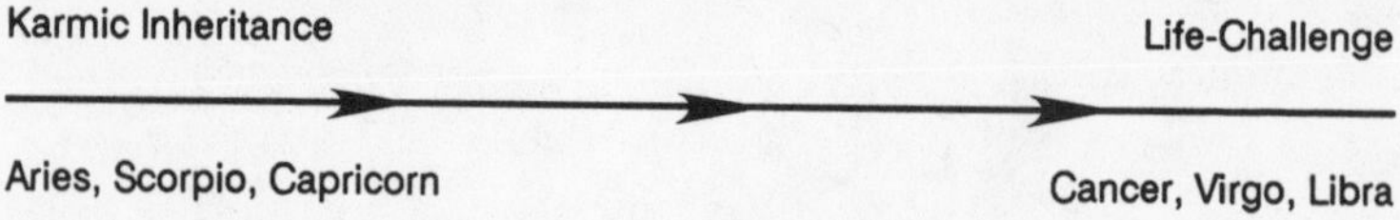

Figure 4. Developmental axis describing growth from an inherited power orientation toward increased sensitivity to others' needs.

way? One relevant issue is selfishness. All of these signs can be concerned with acquiring resources for themselves. They all can be interested in power, or control over their situations and other people. They can all be somewhat harsh or insensitive in this regard. We can see the beginnings of a possible karmic imbalance in the failure to share, cooperate, serve, and be sensitive to others' needs. The person with this inheritance might have the South Node in Aries, in the Eighth House, with Saturn or Moon in Capricorn.

Notice that there are many negative qualities that one or two of these signs might share, but the absence of those qualities in the third rules it out as a theme. For example, Aries and Scorpio might be sexually promiscuous, but Capricorn does not share that trait. Scorpio and Capricorn can be overly controlled and reserved, but Aries certainly is not. Aries and Capricorn can have ambition for social recognition, whereas Scorpio (though capable of worldly success) is usually more subtle and complex in motivation.

On the challenge end of the axis are signs which are more concerned with the welfare of others. Let us say that our hypothetical example includes North Node in Libra, a Cancer Ascendant, and Jupiter in Virgo. Cancer can be nurturing, Virgo service-oriented, and Libra cooperative. These signs are all somewhat sensitive to the feelings of others. Rather than being oriented toward power—or control—Cancer can be vulnerable and dependent, Virgo quite humble, and Libra compromising. We can't say that they're emotionally warm since Virgo is more typically businesslike. We can't say that they're pragmatic, since Libra can be quite indulgent and ineffectual. We can't describe them as rational and objective, since Cancer is emotionally biased.

In summary, we have an individual whose karmic inheritance (imbalance) shows insensitivity, selfishness in the struggle for acquisition, and a desire for power over others. The life-challenge is to be more sensitive and service-oriented toward others. To aid in the fulfillment of this karmic need, the individual inherits the positive qualities (from Aries, Scorpio, and Capricorn) of strength and straightforward communication. Initially, this person may express the life-challenge with great insecurity, a cold, distant interpersonal style, and an overly conventional perspective.

The theme will be filled out by several more factors, as we take into account aspects, Lunation Phase, house placements, etc. Before we progress to full sample charts, it might be good to look at several more examples of abbreviated developmental axes (figures 5–8). These combinations are taken from actual charts. Since I have already made an analysis of the full chart, the interpretations will be informed by internal consistency with the rest of the factors in the chart.

The general theme in figure 5 on page 68 is the universalizing and socializing of personal energy. This person has placed too much emphasis on satisfying individual needs and building a secure foundation. It is now time for growth in the direction of responsible relationships and concern for issues at the societal level. The inheritance brings positive qualities of a simple, child-like openness to experience and a creative, aesthetic, imaginative artistic

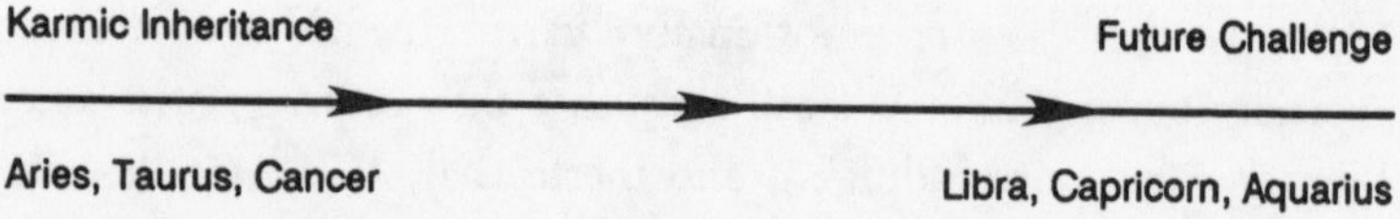

Karmic Inheritance   **Future Challenge**

Aries, Taurus, Cancer   **Libra, Capricorn, Aquarius**

Figure 5.   Example of a developmental axis showing universalization and socialization of personal energy.

sense. Initially, this individual may express the challenge with aloofness, coldness, and impersonality.

Figure 6 shows us an individual with many factors anchored in Gemini and Aquarius. We can determine that this person's background has been one of airy, emotional distance and a rigidly scientific, intellectual approach to life. The inheritance suggests a need for warmth, enthusiasm, passion, and instinctive self-expression. This individual needs "juicier" relationships. The inheritance includes positive traits of the potential for high mental achievement and good communication skills. Imperfect expression of the life-challenge might take the form of sexual promiscuity, arrogance, and insensitivity to others' feelings.

The karmic transition shown in figure 7 is a movement from overly conservative conventionality to creative individuality and risk of transformation. The signs at the left end of the axis

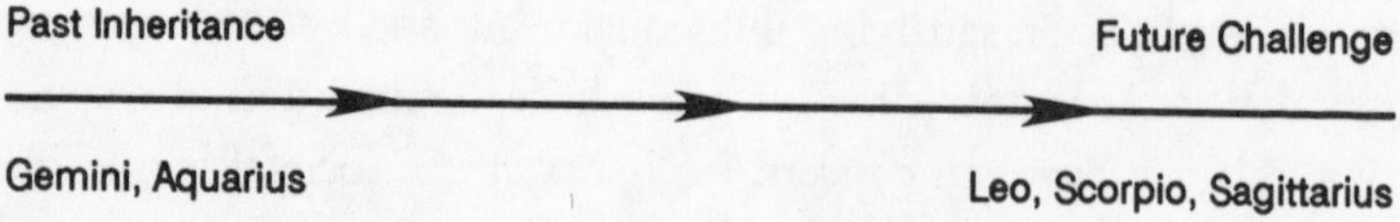

Past Inheritance   **Future Challenge**

Gemini, Aquarius   **Leo, Scorpio, Sagittarius**

Figure 6.   This developmental axis suggests a need for warmth, enthusiasm, passion, and instinctive self-expression.

Figure 7. Example of a developmental axis indicating a movement from conventionality to individuality.

describe relationships that are rooted in tradition: family, marriage, and state. This person is being challenged to be assertive through creative and progressive ideas, and to surrender to the process of death and rebirth as a means of radical growth. The signs in the inheritance indicate that the individual might have developed a high capacity for material success and a refined, dignified demeanor. Reaching for the challenge, this person initially may be excessively critical and insensitive to others' feelings.

The major theme in figure 8 is the "melting" of a power-control orientation into a more sensitive, flowing style of consciousness. The individual's over-concern with practical achievement and the desire for recognition are being modified by the pull toward inward, psychic awareness, domesticity, and compassionate service to other beings. Scorpio, along with the other

Figure 8. This developmental axis indicates a "melting" of power-control into a more sensitive consciousness.

water signs, requires deep emotional relationship as a counter-force to the relative dryness of the signs on the left end of the developmental axis. This individual might bring forward a strong, disciplined will, with a keen moral sense. The challenge may be expressed in the early stages as a moody, chaotic emotional nature and an overly reserved, cautious style.

6

Horoscope Interpretation

Although chart interpretation relies on the creativity and skill of the astrologer, I have developed a method that enables him or her to draw inevitable general conclusions quickly. I begin by examining two major factors: the *structural dimension* (the placement of the factors along the developmental axis) and the *content dimension* (the straightforward symbolic meaning of each factor). I first make notes about the karmic structure of the chart, taking into consideration sign positions, house positions, aspects, Lunation Phase, etc. I usually pull out a couple of "cookbooks" and look up all the placements and aspects. This stimulates my mind and keeps me from forgetting an important slant on the interpretation. It also helps prevent "blindspots," and frees my attention to engage in the all-important synthetic process of discovering the themes which unify, and account for, all the separate factors in the chart. Next, I work to make the overall theme of the chart more and more specific by summarizing the Sabian Symbols for each factor in the chart and synthesizing them into karmic inheritance and life-challenge.

In this chapter I delineate actual horoscopes to demonstrate this approach. The interpretations are somewhat general as I am attempting to present an overall thematic picture and do not wish to "clutter" that picture with too many details at this stage. Hopefully, after reading several delineations, you will see the coherence of the approach. Although I don't adhere rigidly to the sequence in a machine-like way, I generally follow an interpretive order. For instance, I check the challenge-factors first since they are usually more straightforward: North Node of the Moon, Midheaven, Ascendant, retrograde planets. In this group, I look for a preliminary theme. Simply by considering the signs opposite this challenge-group, I may be able to get some ideas about the inheritance theme. I look to the major factors such as South Node, Saturn, Moon, Lunation Phase, and Part of Fortune to see if there is duplication of themes and, therefore, an emphasis in some direction. Finally, after I have completed a thorough examination along these lines and formed a hypothetical developmental axis, I consider the Sabian Symbols of the New Moons and all the other factors to see if these confirm my suppositions or suggest a shift of direction.

The sample horoscopes represent a very important part of this text. They also require the most concentration. It is necessary that you take the time to fully comprehend each chart. It is my recommendation that you not begin reading any text until you have memorized the corresponding horoscope (so you can focus on the interpretive synthesis), and have attempted to identify the past inheritance and life-challenge. (Also, I suggest you use my procedure of looking up all placements and aspects to stimulate your awareness of alternate interpretations. This preparation will not only make the delineation more interesting, it will result in a much more fruitful reading. Finally, I suggest that you refer back to figure 3 on page 33, along with the fuller explanations of each factor in chapter 3, if I come to a conclusion

that puzzles you. If I do not follow a general principle in attrib-
uting signs to the inheritance and challenge, I will try to account
for my reasoning.

Albert Schweitzer

We could describe this man as having been "called to action." He
has a tremendously dynamic chart, shown on page 74, with the
majority of factors falling in cardinal signs, and several major
configurations including a fixed grand cross, a kite, and a number of T-squares.

Schweitzer's inheritance is mutability, which is an evaluative
function. He spent the first 38 years of his life studying, his
interests ranging from music to medicine to philosophy to theol-
ogy, and was a minister in his early adult life. At the age of 21 he
decided that it was neither enough to have studied and considered the meaning of life nor to have given truly inspirational
sermons to his congregation. (Study and communication are
typical manifestations of mutability.) He decided to put his
understanding into action by establishing a medical mission in
the jungles of Africa.

The hardships of his chosen way of life were tremendous,
but the fixed grand cross provided him with the self-sufficiency,
determination, and patience to cope with the conditions he faced.
(Remember that mutable signs tend toward scatteredness, escapism, and impracticality, and these tendencies are being challenged here). The cardinal angles, along with the Sun and Moon
in cardinal signs, gave him the powerful purpose he needed to
combat the natives' resistance to modern ideas.

The focal points of the T-squares show Capricorn characteristics. They also are involved in quintile aspects. Schweitzer used
great creativity in forming and maintaining the structure of his

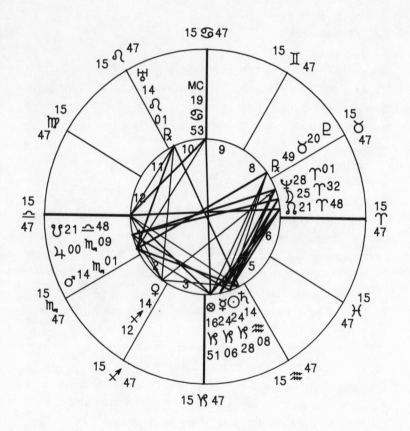

Chart 1.   Albert Schweitzer. He was born January 14, 1875, at 11:50 PM, in Kayersburg, Alsace. Data from Lois Rodden, The American Book of Charts *(San Diego, CA: Astro Computing Services, 1980). Chart calculated by ACS using Equal Houses.*

medical community. The vision of his work remained steady, and, slowly but surely, he built an effective facility which endured through the years.

Marjoe Gortner

The challenges in Chart 2 on page 76 include the retrograde planets in Gemini, Leo, Libra, and Capricorn. The Midheaven is in Aries. The Lunar Phase is an aspect corresponding to Sagittarius.[1] Important planetary placements in the Second, Sixth, and Eleventh Houses suggest Taurus, Virgo, and Aquarius as challenging signs.

This leaves us with a hypothetical inheritance of Cancer, Scorpio, and Pisces. The Moon is in a stressed position at the focal point of a T-square. Gortner was trained to fulfill his frustrated mother's own obsession to become an evangelist. She drilled complicated sermons into his memory from the time he was four years old, and he was punished if he balked. He crisscrossed the country for nine years, achieving fame as a child evangelist. His parents, especially his father, gained financially from his preaching. The adult-like responsibility he bore in his childhood seemed to be the manifestation of his heavily afflicted Moon. Also, his mother was the primary source of indoctrination and discipline. At one time in his life, when he felt greatly exploited, he asked, "Did you ever love me, Mother?" Cancer seems to be an important part of the inheritance.

The Part of Fortune is in Pisces in the Eighth House. Both Pluto and Neptune are integrated into the chart in many ways, and both have a mixture of less- and more-stressed aspects. Even more important than these qualities is the fact that the all-water

---

[1]See Bill Tierney, *Dynamics of Aspect Analysis* (Sebastopol, California: CRCS Publications, 1983), p. 30.

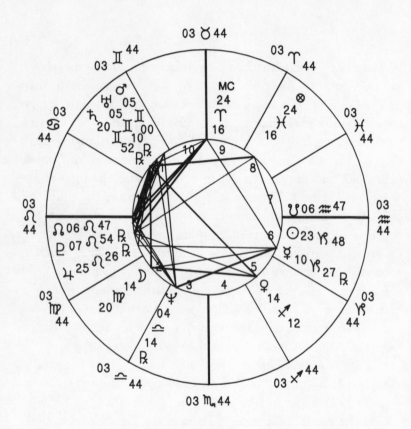

*Chart 2.   Marjoe Gortner. He was born January 14, 1944, at 6:49
PM, in Long Beach, CA. Data from Lois Rodden,* The American
Book of Charts *(San Diego, CA: Astro Computing Services, 1980).
Chart calculated by ACS using Equal Houses.*

inheritance makes sense. Gortner's strength as a preacher was his uncanny ability to size up an audience and use his considerable powers of emotional persuasion to manipulate a response from the congregation. He is very sensitive and has a genuine psychic power to heal, a demonstration of which never failed to elicit a good financial response.

Marjoe Gortner's challenge is to bring the depth and the visionary qualities of the psychic inheritance into practical reality. He has the mental and verbal ability of Gemini, the self-expression of Aries, the dramatic talent of Leo, and the earth-element emphasis that would enable him to manifest his ideals in an effective, tangible way.

Grandma Moses

The horoscope of Grandma Moses is shown as Chart 3 on page 78. Let's consider the challenging factors first. We can include the retrograde planets in Pisces and Taurus. We have the angles, Scorpio and Capricorn. We have the Sun sign, Virgo. With the North Node in the First House, and Mars on the Ascendant, we can include Aries. With three factors in Leo, and Moon and Uranus in the Fifth House, I would make Leo part of the challenge. North Node in challenging Aquarius supports a Moon-Uranus conjunction. If we assume the rest of the signs belong to the inheritance (except for Sagittarius, which we will put into the challenge-group), this leaves us with the developmental axis shown in figure 9 on page 79.

If we consider the Cancer factor, we see a variety of direct opposition-challenges to the Moon. The Moon Phase itself is a Capricorn factor (upper square), there is an upper square from the Moon to Saturn, and the Moon makes an exact sesquiquadrate to the Capricorn Ascendant. The Moon is also complexly

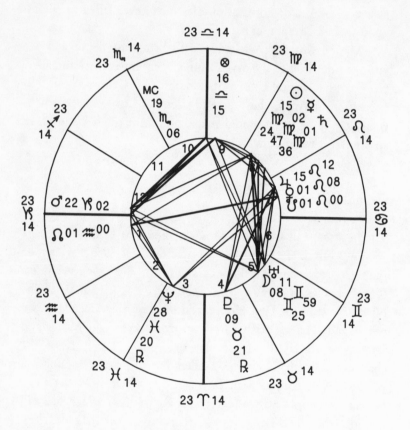

Chart 3.   Grandma Moses (Anna Mary Robertson). She was born September 7, 1860, at 3:58 PM, in Greenwich, NY. Data from Lois Rodden, Profiles of Women *(Tempe, AZ: American Federation of Astrologers, 1979). Chart calculated By ACS using Equal Houses.*

Figure 9.   Developmental axis for Chart 3.

integrated into the chart with its many aspects. Grandma Moses' life reflects the Cancerian emphasis on home and family. She was a member of a large family, was devoted to her parents and siblings, and worked as a "domestic" until she was married in her mid-twenties. The Fourth House (a Cancer factor) is widely considered the ruler of the farm environment, where she spent her entire life. After marrying, she raised a large family.

The Part of Fortune is in Libra, the Seventh House is heavily tenanted, and Venus is receiving a direct opposition-challenge from Mars. Grandma Moses had a profound sensitivity to beauty from early childhood. She had a remarkable visual memory of the way things looked, especially landscapes. She saved (Cancer) pretty things from the summer so she could admire them in the winter. Early in her life she had a facility for drawing and painting.

Gemini, as an inheritance factor, is supported by the placements of the Moon and Uranus there (break out of the limitations of the sign). More importantly, I like the coherency of its inclusion in the inheritance-group. This woman lived in a narrow environment, which included her parents, siblings, husband, children, and immediate neighbors. She showed little of the wandering inclination of Sagittarius until later in her life when she did some traveling. The Part of Fortune is in the Ninth House and Jupiter is only a moderately integrated planet in the chart, so I tend to place it in the challenge-group.

If we consider a synthesis of the three inherited energies— Gemini, Cancer, and Libra—we see an individual with strong social loyalty and attunement to the needs of others. On the negative side, there is a tendency toward a narrow perspective and to be limited to the politics of the immediate social environment. This individual was dependent upon being accepted by others and had difficulty asserting herself.

Anna Mary Robertson (Grandma Moses' maiden name) was undoubtedly a very cooperative child, devoted wife, and nurturing mother to her children. Her destiny was to express herself artistically in such a way that she brought the organic simplicity and purity of her lifestyle to the world. This required challenges of self-assertiveness (Aries factors), creative self-expression (Leo), ambition (Capricorn), independence (Aries and Aquarius), and development of technique (Virgo). The Scorpio Midheaven helped her to get down to the essentials in her artwork, and gave her the emotional intensity and power to bring her talent to the world. Though it took her until seventy years of age, Grandma Moses overcame the social responsibilities she had taken on and surrendered to the powerful urge to manifest her appreciation of nature, which brought her fame and gratitude from a wide range of people.

Paul Newman

Chart 4 is an example of someone who expressed his challenge fairly early in life due to the high-impact placement of these challenging factors. Capricorn dominates the Ascendant area, the heavily tenanted First House adds Aries, and Aquarius rounds out this part of the challenge with Sun, Part of Fortune, and South Node in this sign. Saturn and the Midheaven, along with Neptune and North Node in the Eighth, make Scorpio a challenge factor. Jupiter and Mercury conjunct the Ascendant add Sagittarius and Virgo to the list (Sabian Symbols support

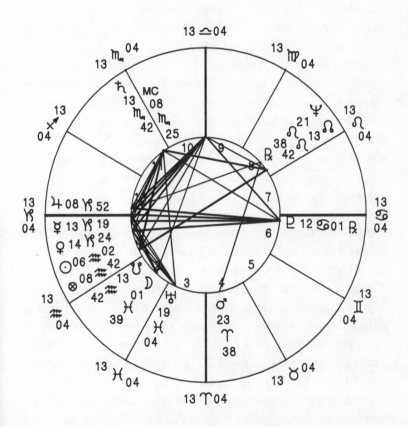

Chart 4. Paul Newman. He was born January 26, 1925, at 6:30 AM, in Cleveland, OH. Data from Lois Rodden, The American Book of Charts (San Diego, CA: Astro Computing Services, 1980). Chart calculated by ACS using Equal Houses.

Mercury-ruled Virgo rather than Gemini as a challenge). Neptune retrograde and North Node, both in Leo, make a challenge. Pluto retrograde, combined with Mars in the Fourth, indicate that Cancer is also in the challenge-group. Finally, South Node and Moon in the Second, along with the semi-sextile Moon Phase, suggest Taurus' inclusion in the challenge-group. The developmental axis now looks like figure 10.

By process of elimination, the inheritance-group is composed of Gemini, Libra, and Pisces. This fits Paul Newman's character and life in many ways. First of all, his strongest interest—and one for which he showed promise—was acting (Pisces is a co-ruler of acting and films, along with Leo). He took part in plays from grade school through college. And, when he was pressured to take over his father's lucrative sporting goods business (business was his college major), he hated every minute of the time he spent studying, and participating in, this activity. Shortly after his father died, he quit the business, headed for Yale Drama School, and then on to New York to act on the stage. Shortly thereafter, he went to Hollywood to star in the movies. This was an inheritance asserting itself strongly!

In addition to the number of aspects to Venus (including afflictions from Mars and Neptune), there is plenty of evidence that Paul Newman has Libra as an inheritance. He usually has handled himself with grace in his personal and business relationships. He is described as "beautiful" by both his mother and wife. Atypical of Hollywood movie stars, his married life has been a relatively stable one. He is considered one of the more

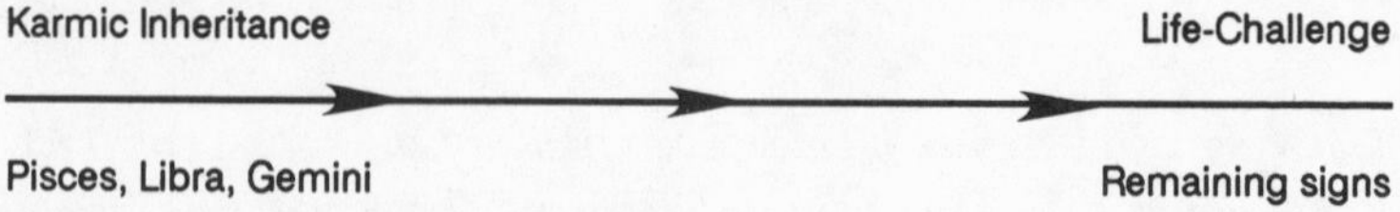

Karmic Inheritance   **Life-Challenge**

→   →   →

Pisces, Libra, Gemini   Remaining signs

Figure 10.   Developmental axis for Chart 4.

"balanced" personalities in Hollywood. Also, despite powerful Aries and Scorpio challenges, they did not assert themselves as his passion for race-car driving until later in his life. Without the artistic and refined Libra factor, I believe the competitiveness and instinctual adventurousness would have inclined him to racing much earlier.

While Newman's reputation is of an actor with somewhat limited scope, he is considered quite intelligent by his peers. He loves to research his roles and thoroughly studies any subject which interests him. He likes to read, and corresponds with many people whom he respects in various fields. Hence, Gemini fits as an inherited quality.

As a group, the inheritance factors can be synthesized if we consider the lack of fixed, fire, and earth energies, as well as the relative loss of identity suggested by the Libra energy. Altogether, it can mean confusion, passivity, and irresponsibility regarding his practical role in the world. Indeed, Newman did some drifting and some "selling out" of his deeper personal goals, mostly to please his family and out of insecurity. Only after his father's death, and with the support of his wife, did he have the courage to enter Yale Drama School to study the acting he loved at about age twenty-six. Even after he became a movie star, it was years before he felt financially secure due to his lack of savvy in the more practical areas.

On the positive side, these inherited signs gave Newman the imagination, sensitivity, and depth that he needed to be a successful actor, and the charisma to affect millions of people as a "star."

Paul Newman's challenge contains three major themes: one is self-directedness and individuality; another somewhat associated theme is the development of his sense of pathos and personal power; a final one is stability.

The first theme is described by the predominance of planets on the eastern side of the chart, especially the First House (Aries) factors, and Aquarius placements. These are powerful, immediate inducements to developing independence, which progressively characterizes this man's life and thinking.

Newman's more mature roles, especially in *Hud*, demonstrate his capacity for the intensity, darkness, and coldness of Scorpio and Capricorn.

Finally, the extent of the fixed challenge, along with Capricorn, brought him the stamina, steadiness, and determination required to overcome the self-indulgence and "flakiness" which characterized an early period in his career (when he was very reactive and prone to excessive drinking). Also, Mercury is at the release point of a kite formation and, since it forms nearly an exact conjunction to the Ascendant, it can serve as a strong, clarifying influence on the mind.

Grace Kelly

The first thing I notice about Grace Kelly's chart (Chart 5 on page 85) is the amount of challenging Scorpio energy. Three planets, including the Sun and the Ascendant, are in the sign. Pluto is the most elevated planet in the chart and part of a grand trine with the Sun and Moon. Also, Jupiter is calling for an expansion of Scorpio energy by its position in the Eighth House, completing a heavy, multi-faceted emphasis of this sign.

As usual, I put the Midheaven's sign, Leo, into the challenge category, along with the signs which contain retrograde planets: Aries, Gemini, and Cancer. The Part of Fortune and Moon in the Fifth House, in addition to the Lower Trine Moon

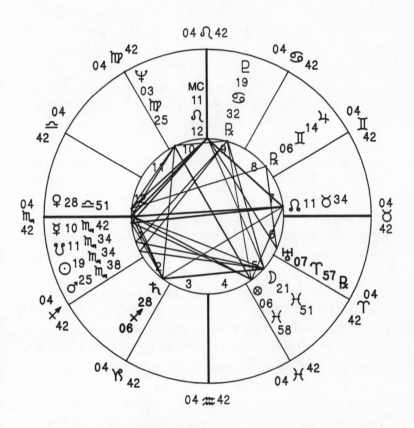

Chart 5. Grace Kelly. She was born November 12, 1929 at 5:31 AM, in Philadelphia, PA. Data from Lois Rodden, Profiles of Women *(Tempe, AZ: American Federation of Astrologers, 1979). Chart calculated by ACS using Equal Houses.*

Phase, confirm the Leo challenge. The stellium in the First House and Mars conjunct Sun support the Aries theme.

When I see Kelly's Moon and Part of Fortune in Pisces, I wonder to myself if they are inheritance factors. It is feasible, considering the number of aspects to Neptune, so I note that. When I look at Saturn, I wonder the same thing about Sagittarius. Jupiter is adversely aspected and Pluto is transforming the Ninth House.

Venus near the Ascendant in Libra, along with a Taurus North Node in the Seventh, and Saturn in the Second House, leads me to believe both Venus-ruled energies are challenges.

Mercury, midway between the Ascendant and Sun, stimulates the idea that Virgo is a challenge (Uranus is also being put to work in the Sixth). We already have concluded that Gemini falls in the challenge-group.

Saturn is strongly challenging the Moon, and since Neptune looks to be structured by the Tenth House (Neptune retrogrades back further into the Tenth House by progression), we can surmise that Capricorn is a challenge.

This leaves Aquarius as a final consideration. Uranus is at the focal point of a Yod, an important configuration. With only Sagittarius and Pisces as inheritance factors so far, perhaps we can hypothesize this trio as our karmic group, with the rest of the energies as challenges (see figure 11).

My task now is to synthesize the three energies we hypothesized for the inheritance and see how they could explain Grace Kelly's early life. In an abstract sense, they are universal energies

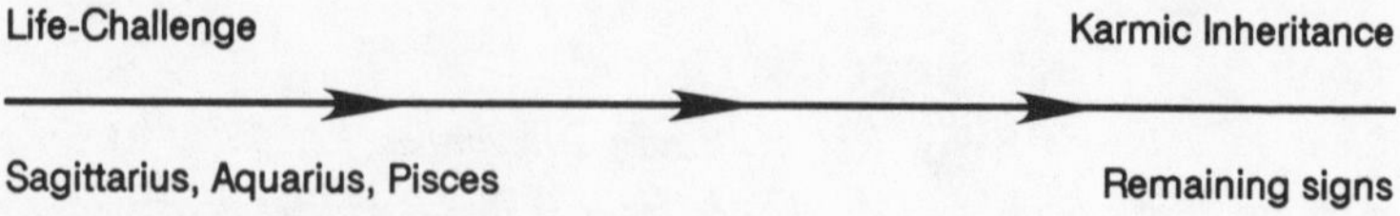

Life-Challenge   Karmic Inheritance

Sagittarius, Aquarius, Pisces   Remaining signs

Figure 11.   Developmental axis for Chart 5.

(as distinct from personal and social), freedom-oriented, creative, and with an awareness of group process and higher ideals. We would expect these energies to manifest as broad social concern, popularity, and a certain development of imagination and wisdom. On the negative side, there may be a lack of practicality, an absence of stability, and little commitment in relationships.

At this point in my analysis, I typically refer to the Sabian Symbols to verify or disprove my hypotheses. In this case, I feel I am borne out by a consistent reference to the need for a down-to-earth, everyday practicality. There are many references to the concrete manifestation of values and ideals. Development of potential into overt self-expression is emphasized. There is the general theme of a background of universal energy which needs to be made functional in ordinary relationships and responsibilities.

As a child, Grace Kelly was meek, sickly, and ethereal. She spent much time in fantasy, playing make-believe with her dolls. Individuals with lots of universal energy in the inheritance are frequently "out of place" as young children. Kelly faded into the background in her family of outgoing, athletic, assertive individuals. One day a sister led her into a closet and left her in there all day. She contentedly amused herself with her active imagination. Kelly seemed passively detached from her siblings and playmates, and did not demand the kind of attention many youngsters do. She was popular enough in school, however, and became much more so when she reached her teens.

Acting, which required the kind of universal sympathy represented by the Pisces energy in her chart, came naturally to her. At the age of nine or ten, she was already interested in acting, and by twelve, she was performing regularly with an acting troupe. She instinctively knew how to communicate a role to an audience, so success came to her steadily and surely.

As she grew to womanhood, her personal life reflected the qualities of this inheritance as well. She had the depth and breadth to be able to get along with everyone. Every leading man seemed to fall in love with her and she reciprocated in what many felt was a promiscuous way. She seemed to lack discrimination: most of these relationships, while substantive, did not offer permanence, either because the man was married, or she didn't love him, or her family was dead set against him. She had a soft spot for individuals with artistic or literary talents — the more romantic the better. She also enjoyed mental challenges and language games, such as those she shared with Alfred Hitchcock.

Throughout Kelly's acting career, during which she achieved great popularity and critical esteem, and during her marriage to Prince Ranier of Monaco, which may have drawn more attention than that of any couple in history, her universal inheritance was being expressed. (Obviously, her acting career also expressed Leo, a challenging energy.)

A major theme of Grace Kelly's challenge was the demand for intimate relationship (Libra and Scorpio). It was as though her emotional responses were so scattered that the focus of emotional-sexual involvement was the necessary remedy. The Scorpio emphasis accounted for the dichotomy between the poised, controlled, almost icy elegance she projected and her very sexual, almost slutty, reputation. The courageous fulfillment of this relationship challenge came when on relatively short notice and with little preparation, she took the step to become the Princess of Monaco. Her husband was such a rigid traditionalist, and the demands of her role so circumscribed, that this life became one of tremendous discipline and restraint. In stark contrast to the variety of relationships and circumstances available in her screen roles, she had to serve her husband and her subjects.

The other challenge presented her by this marriage was that of mother (Cancer and Leo). Producing an heir for the Prince (which was necessary if Monaco was to remain an independent state) was so crucial a requirement that Kelly had to undergo a fertility test in order to "qualify" for the marriage. Leo on her Midheaven underscored the fact that motherhood was one of her main "jobs." (It should be noted that Leo also rules royalty.) Indeed, she took it so seriously that she studied natural childbirth and childrearing extensively, eventually becoming an important figure in the La Leche movement.

Another challenge was the translation of her transcendental wisdom, high ideals, and need to serve humanity (universal inheritance) into concrete, everyday practicality. She expressed this through managing the palace staff and planning royal activities. She organized functions where honored dignitaries of state were received, took part in activities in support of charitable organizations, and prepared for participation in other official occasions. This required her to use her earth qualities of discipline, planning, and attention to detail.

While her life as Princess Grace took her to even greater heights of popularity and world interest (a carry-over of her universal inheritance), it required a tremendous amount of character development to fulfill successfully. Although she remained married for many years and raised two daughters and a son to carry on the royal tradition, she suffered much frustration. Her husband and the people of Monaco revolted whenever she expressed a desire to take another film role. She also experienced loneliness and pain. It took her a long time to adjust to the formality of palace life, and in later years she frequently used alcohol and food as means of escape.

7

The Birthchart as a Tool in Counseling

I believe the crucial variable to address when counseling someone is responsible relationship, by which I mean the person's ability to be intimate with others. It is my opinion that an individual's level of conscious development can be ascertained by observing how responsible that individual is in relationships — a phrase which implies many qualities.

As responsible individuals, we understand our own natures — the weaknesses (sins of both omission and commission) inherent in being human, as well as the strengths — and attempt to deal with them through conscious effort and discipline. We recognize the human condition as a profound and serious one, and are oriented toward a process of growth, enlightenment, and real happiness. Possessed of this understanding, we are naturally tolerant of the imperfection of ourselves and others so that we are capable of compassionate love and effective service to other human beings.

I feel that an extremely important factor in developing the capacity for responsible relationship is awareness of our own karmic tendencies. If I am becoming aware of my karmic inheritance, and the myriad and subtle ways it is expressed in my everyday behavior, it is more likely that I am humbled and impressed by the need for personal transformation and more disposed to treat with real love those around me who are all coping with the same general nature.

There are a number of available approaches which can help individuals become aware of their limitations and which encourage responsible adaptation. My educational, professional, and personal background as a clinical psychologist has exposed me to many of them. My general impression is that their concepts are limited. Being unfamiliar with the notion of karma, most psychological approaches are geared to finding a specific cause or origin in the personal past for the client's problems. The belief is that by identifying this problem, the individual will be liberated. Too few approaches acknowledge the need for new behavior as an important supplement to any insight-giving process that also may be engaged. Nor do most fields of psychological thought have a spiritual foundation or acknowledge a Higher Self.

Another limitation of most therapies is their narrow perspective: they attempt to fit everyone into a homogeneous "normal zone" of self-expression and behavior. They have little appreciation for the profound differences in energy patterns among individuals. Also, these approaches utilize hit-or-miss diagnostic procedures; they depend upon confession as the principle means of identifying the individual's problems and tendencies. Because most people's defense systems work to conceal problems and limitations, extensive personal observation is often necessary before the counselor can comprehend those limitations fully.

While astrology and the psychic arts acknowledge concepts such as karma and reincarnation, they focus largely upon the past and the causal roots of behavior. Few people acknowledge, or know how to recognize, the graceful impetus toward challenging growth which the universe provides. Therefore, astrological and psychic readings often are fateful and defensive in tone. Metaphysical counselors tend to encourage people to accept their karmic "destiny" or to resolve their karmic limitations without showing them what resources they have to accomplish this.

It seems to me, therefore, that my life-challenge approach provides a tool for effective counseling. I have demonstrated its power as a diagnostic method for identifying the karmic inheritance. Also, I have outlined a perspective which describes a natural direction of growth for the individual. This challenging pattern of energies represents the most efficient compensation for the karmic imbalances which have accumulated. This information enables each of us to take responsibility for our own development. We can consider how the challenging themes are being expressed in our lives and attempt to overcome any resistance to expanding these energies. Once we understand our own tendencies we can be more tolerant of others, and can enter into relationships honestly.

How can the astrologer best communicate this information to the client? Although "diagnostic" reading can be a most important impetus to a person's growth, a one-shot in-depth astrological analysis is frequently overwhelming. Many clients have trouble assimilating so much material in one dose.

Let's consider the nature of a human being's psychological defense system. We all have a "shadow" side to our egos: images and feelings which describe us in a very unflattering light. We are vaguely aware of some of them and are struggling to repress, deny, or transcend them. Others we have not allowed ourselves to notice. To bring this material to light is to "lose face." The ego is struggling to survive by keeping its "face" invulnerable, perfect, and socially acceptable. Most of us are capable of behavior which is not consistent with this "face," even though we like to believe we are in control of ourselves. To acknowledge that there are aspects of ourselves that we have not mastered indicates we are not in control. This reminds us that we are extremely vulnerable in the universe as separate individuals and thus arouses fear.

A more subtle perspective, which was hinted at earlier, is that the "face" of the individual implies an element of control of one's "destiny." In order to maintain a good face, a person has to adopt a habit of contraction in order to avoid certain reactions or situations which will elicit these reactions. In this sense, to break down this contraction by exposure to material from the "shadow" side is to break down the ego. What is so threatening about this? Basically, we are weak-willed, indiscriminate, undisciplined, morally confused people. If we allow these tendencies and impulses to surface, we are likely to act on them, especially if we have little understanding of an alternative, spiritually-transcending recourse. Better to remain unaware of them and be safe from the personal and social consequences of "wild" or "crazy" or truly destructive behavior.

In addition, a tremendous karmic history is being summarized in each individual's consciousness. We grow and change slowly and the suffering of unenlightened existence is exacerbated by our own resistance (indeed, our resistance is our suffering). Becoming aware of the depth of our karmic limitations can be discouraging. It is no superficial fault that we ordinarily have no memory of previous lives. We need forgiveness of self and fresh starts to sustain our growth.

When first developing this approach, I was very concerned with validation. In my zeal, I would tell clients everything I knew about their horoscopes in order to get some feedback regarding accuracy. What I found was that this approach produced interpretations which could be disturbing to some people.

In fact, it was hard for me to evaluate some of the readings in the beginning because I wasn't sure whether my clients' reactions were due to incorrect interpretations or to correct ones. Eventually, I realized that most people were coping with anxiety aroused by deep feelings of recognition of their karmic inheritances. Some individuals began talking a lot to distract me from continuing the presentation; others became silent and slightly rigid. One woman confessed she nearly got up and walked out when I presented the negative side of the inheritance.

In general, however, I never had the feeling that disclosing this information did anyone any harm in the long run. Even in those few instances where they were defensive, people were typically appreciative of the readings and their defense systems adequately coped with the material presented to them. Most of my clients—many of whom had been given previous astrological and psychic readings—felt that they received the most far-reaching understanding of their lives.

Naturally, I welcomed corroboration of my interpretations, but more importantly, I was pleased that this information had value in my clients' development. This perspective is so pervasive that it takes awhile to realize we are living expressions of the horoscope symbology. The knowledge that we need to transcend certain energies and more intimately identify with others is helpful even in a day-to-day sense. It gives us an intelligent basis for self-discipline and "right action," a term from karma yoga. Meeting one's life-challenge is not a sufficient basis for spiritual growth—this involves higher principles beyond the scope of this volume. Doing so does prepare us at the human level, however, to balance ourselves as a prelude to the higher processes.

Considering the value and potency of the information available in the life-challenge approach, it is important that we astrologers deliver our understanding in a way that results in maximum benefits for our clients. Astrology is primarily a conceptual system, though it relies on intuitive and psychic impulses as secondary factors. The symbols, their inter-relationships, and their cycles of motion provide an objective and abstract structure upon which to overlay the rich variety of human experience. Astrology's conceptual magnificence sometimes can lure us into an insensitivity when communicating our understanding to lay-people. Sometimes our fascination with the facile gems of interpretation can become more important than the education of the client. To those of us who are astrologers, our study is inherently valuable and useful in a personal sense, but we must remember that most of us are being challenged, through our understanding, to serve and enlighten others. Mastering the horoscope is only the first step. Interaction with our clients is the next, and equally important, part of the process.

An extremely gentle approach to communicating information to a client, which some may prefer, is one central to gestalt therapy. It is that we must assimilate truth as a natural extension of our own awareness. We don't swallow food whole; rather, we digest it slowly and make it a part of our bodies through intimate contact with our digestive systems. A gestalt therapist elicits awareness of ourselves first, then directs our awareness in such a way that we're likely to gain further insight through the natural processes of growth. Basically, the therapist makes a judgment regarding the status of the awareness material in the framework of a hypothesized gestalt. Gestalts have a natural tendency to complete themselves, to progress from the negative state of deprivation, or imbalance, to the positive one of satisfaction, regaining of homeostasis, and completion.

In astrological readings, clients' awareness of their own karmic gestalts can be evaluated through questions about their perception of their own karmic states, limitations, or aspirations. Questions such as: "What areas of life give you the most difficulty?" "What general lessons do you feel you are here to learn?"

"What qualities would you like to develop that are not presently strong in you?" would provide a sound basis for transmission of information in a reading. Material which is closest to the client's self-concept has the greatest chance of being assimilated. The astrologer then can gauge the client's acceptance of initial astrological interpretations and decide what else to bring out. I am not implying that an astrologer should not tell clients anything which offends them. It is sometimes helpful for individuals to be confronted with aspects of themselves that are negative. It is, rather, the emotional environment in which this is done that is most important.

Another suggestion is to emphasize the life-challenge in the early part of the reading, focusing on the positive qualities that need strengthening. The inheritance is implied in this approach, and the client will demonstrate a capacity for facing it by asking questions or spontaneously confessing the limitations. The astrologer also can stimulate exploration of the inheritance by asking questions of increasing intensity, taking the client's responses into account as questioning progresses.

Many of us are still struggling to understand our own charts completely (we are always the last to see ourselves objectively). So, it seems a single reading is not sufficient to give a client all the information he or she needs. I suggest more extended contact with clients (two or three meetings in the course of a year) may be necessary before they can fully assimilate, at least at a mental level, material rendered within this approach.

Conclusion

By the time I finished the preparation of this manuscript, I had taught this approach to students in a face-to-face situation. I have begun to realize that reaching the appropriate conclusions is a subtle process. Above all, it takes time, persistence, and tolerance for ambiguity. The many factors in the chart need to be juggled constantly and patiently in your mind's eye until an "Aha!" experience occurs. At this moment you will have progressed from hypothetical hunches and tentative theories to a feeling of assurance that the key themes have been discovered. The main criterion of this discovery is the inclusiveness of the interpretation. Whatever factor you look at in the birthchart, whatever sign position or aspect, its meaning will support the major themes. This internal consistency brightens the horoscope and clarifies the gestalt that is being symbolized.

I hope you have found this material helpful. This book is meant to be a presentation of ideas that need a great deal more research and experience to refine. There is much to be learned regarding the position of each symbol on a time dimension and how recent its contribution is to the karmic themes. I have not discovered yet whether or how aspects to the Nodes indicate if an individual responds to the challenge or regresses into the inheritance. Nor have I determined whether the asteroids can provide more specificity to the karmic axis. It would also be interesting to see the manner in which an individual's development from karmic inheritance to life-challenge unfolds as a result of transits and progressions. I invite you to work with this approach, to expand upon the foundation I have laid. I welcome general responses, as well as findings of those who experiment with this approach. Please contact me through the publisher.